Churchill

An Extraordinary Life

Churchill

An Extraordinary Life

Sarah Gristwood and Margaret Gaskin

National Trust

First published in the United Kingdom in 2019 by
National Trust Books
43 Great Ormond Street
London
WC1N 3HZ

An imprint of Pavilion Books Company Ltd

ISBN 978-1-91135-853-4

A CIP catalogue record for this book is available from the
British Library.

10 9 8 7 6 5 4 3 2 1

Reproduction by Mission Productions Ltd, Hong Kong
Printed in Malaysia by Vivar Printing

This book can be ordered direct from the publisher at
www.pavilionbooks.com

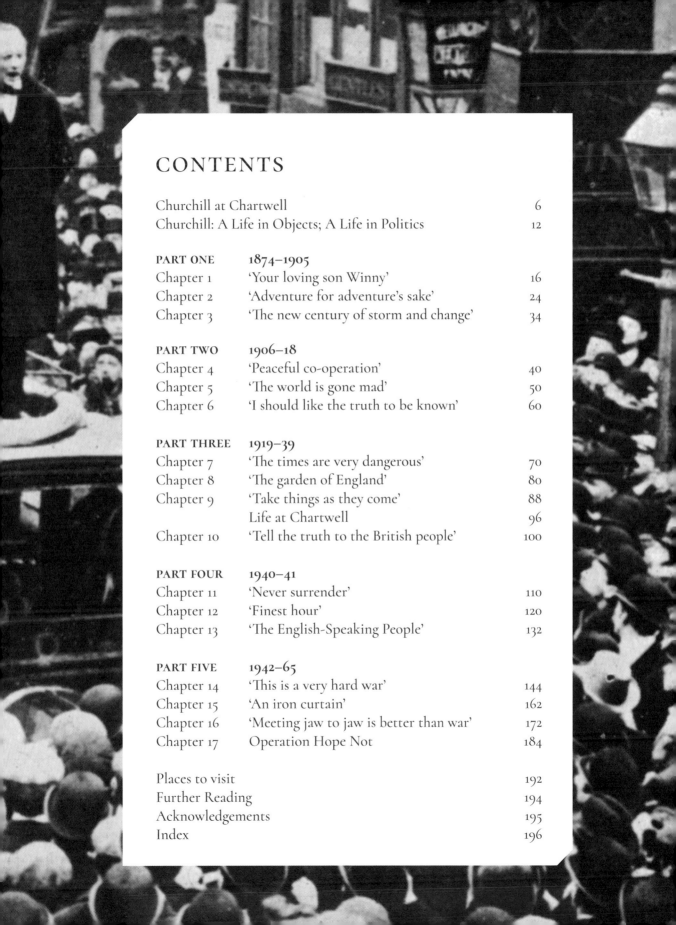

CONTENTS

Churchill at Chartwell

If we were to guess who lived in this home by the objects in it, the study at Chartwell in Kent would not present much of a challenge. One vast bookcase, holding books on every subject but especially history. Above the fireplace, a stained and tattered Union Flag that looks to have seen action. A long lectern for specific books and, off the study, a tiny bedroom – a spartan disregard for sleeping when there is work to be done? Or someone who likes to read in bed?

Moving to the cluttered writing desk, busts of Nelson and Napoleon show an appreciation of both winners and losers in wars. Family photographs include one of a beautiful woman, dated 1940. Examining the pile of 'treasury tags' that keep papers in order without new-fangled staples, the spectacles, the cigar-cutter … we have it: this is the country home of Winston Churchill! The flag was the first British flag to fly over a liberated European capital in 1944, a gift from Field Marshal Alexander; the mahogany lectern a birthday present from his children to replace the plain deal one that served until 1949; that favourite photograph of his wife Clementine, which he later rendered as a painting, shows her launching the aircraft carrier HMS *Indomitable*.

But then, glancing around, the question rises again unbidden: 'Who lives in a house like this?' What about the fish tank bubbling in the corner? The stuffed toys among the history books, one holding in place a biography of Hitler? When, in the late 1940s, a small boy turned up on Churchill's birthday at his London home with a tin of Black Mollies, Winston was thrilled, had the fish sent down to Chartwell and 'got an expert in'; his growing tropical fish collection soon became the indoor equivalent of the beloved golden orfe that he painted so often in the outdoor ponds. And the shabby toys? Typically inventive aides-mémoire so his helpers knew where to replace books after use.

The question has become 'Who *is* Winston Churchill?' He wrote millions of words in this room; many millions more have been written about him (the first biography appeared when he was just 30); he was a performer on the world stage for seven decades. Efforts to shut him up in a tidy package and consign him to the past are in vain – he remains a player, always ready for one last curtain call.

Labour leader Clement Attlee, put on the spot by an obituarist, described his old friend and rival as 'Rather like a layer cake. One layer was certainly seventeenth century. The eighteenth century in him is obvious. There was the nineteenth century, and a large slice, of course, of the twentieth century; and another, curious layer which may possibly have been the twenty-first.'

OPPOSITE: From the study at Chartwell, Churchill and his helpers poured out the millions of words that earned the money to keep the whole show on the road.
RIGHT: Winston loved this photograph of his wife launching a ship – it was one of the photographs he also rendered as a monochrome painting.

From the vantage point of the twenty-first century, we can see Churchill might indeed have something interesting and instructive to say, probably from personal experience, on many of the topics that fill our newspapers and internet forums today. (The tweets of Winston Churchill would be something to behold!) But he would not always come from the angle expected, nor support the side of the controversy that might expect his backing. 'You assume the future is a mere extension of the past,' he wrote to a future Viceroy of India in May 1933, 'whereas I find history full of unexpected turns and retrogressions.'

At the time, Winston Churchill was banished to the political wilderness. But just seven years later, the debate began in the House of Commons that would lead to him becoming Britain's wartime Prime Minister. It was not the first revolution in his fortunes but it was the greatest, elevating him from an always-colourful political and literary character to a world figure seen by many as not just the greatest Englishman of the twentieth century, but the greatest statesman of the modern era.

Others take a different view. Our century has opened up the debate to many voices, from many lands and many perspectives, and Winston Churchill's huge presence took him into many histories where he does not always appear so heroic.

And the long history of memoirs presenting the other side of practically every argument he'd ever had – and there were many – put large issues back into dispute. After the publishing of one such, Clementine said to their doctor, 'You know, Charles, I am not really angry … We must get used to criticism of Winston. I realise the poor darling cannot be a demi-god forever.' All of which Churchill himself, as a historian, would find quite understandable: 'My views,' he once said, 'represent a continual process of adjustment to changing events.' Life had taken him from cavalry charge to atomic age in less than 50 years; he would expect new perspectives to emerge, and he was surprisingly apt to put himself in the other person's shoes once the hurly-burly of debate was done. But he might nevertheless come back with some interesting arguments of his own in the twenty-first century – or even the twenty-second.

OPPOSITE: The painting that hangs over the fireplace shows Churchill's ancestral home of Blenheim. Awareness of his famous forebears played a large role in Winston's life.
ABOVE: As was common among couples of their class, Winston and Clementine kept separate bedrooms; Winston's was part of his working hub.

Having 'done the state some service' (to quote Shakespeare, another Englishman who gleaned 'small Latin and less Greek' from his schooldays) he might also pray:

> Speak of me as I am. Nothing extenuate,
> Nor set down aught in malice. Then must you speak
> Of one that loved not wisely, but too well.

His loves were many: Clemmie and the children; Chartwell; animals of all kinds but especially pigs; good cigars and champagne; history and futurology; his parents; his nanny; the House of Commons; the British Empire … But the 'unexpected turns and retrogressions' of his own strange, eventful political history may best be understood primarily in terms of twin loves of war and of good governance – or at least, his ideal of them.

The war he loved – and his blood, to his shame, would always quicken at the thought of a scrap – was the old notion of a contest of champions from the storybooks. But in 1901, within three months of entering the House of Commons, the 26-year-old battlefield veteran warned MPs: 'The wars of peoples will be more terrible than the wars of kings.' Surprising as it may seem, given his popular image, Churchill spent the rest of his life trying to prevent such wars happening – even if this meant fighting wars to do so.

This is where his infatuation with war got entangled with his lifelong – and often equally problematic – devotion to good governance: what he described in 1946 as 'the safety and welfare, the freedom and progress, of all the homes and families of all the men and women in all the lands.' If he, inwardly, believed Winston Churchill was best judge of how that was to be achieved, he was also passionately committed to the system that kept the impulses of such men as he in check: in 1947, just two years after he was thrown out of office by the votes of the nation he had done so much to save, Churchill spoke no less proudly from the Opposition benches of the House of Commons than he had as Prime Minister.

'Many forms of Government have been tried, and will be tried in this world of sin and woe,' he told his fellow MPs, 'No one pretends that democracy is perfect or all-wise. Indeed, it has been said that democracy is the worst form of Government except all those other forms that have been tried from time to time, but there is the broad feeling in our country that the people should rule … should shape, guide, and control the actions of Ministers who are their servants and not their masters.'

Even when the twenty-first century rolls on into the twenty-second, we may reasonably expect the life story of Winston Churchill to resonate. Not for where he was born – though he was intensely proud of that – but for what he believed in. Nor for everything he believed in, but for what has stood the test of time. Perhaps future ages, too, may judge: 'He was a man, take him for all in all.'

Certainly, we shall not look upon his like again.

OPPOSITE: The long lectern held the various books Churchill was consulting on a particular project, which was usually dictated to a loyal team of secretaries.
BELOW: Winston Churchill joins the King and Queen and Princesses on the balcony of Buckingham Palace on VE Day for a moment of collective national elation.

Churchill: A Life in Objects

For more than 40 years Chartwell was Winston Churchill's family home and the place of his heart. Today the house, the gardens and the objects preserved there provide visitors with unique, intimate access to the extraordinary life of this complex figure who came to dominate his times.

1 HIS MOTHER One of the dominant influences of Winston's life – adored, but all too often absent – is here sketched by the leading portrait painter John Singer Sargent. The beautiful Jennie Jerome was the first of the 'Dollar Princesses', American heiresses who stormed British high society. Winston's schoolboy letters often pleaded in vain for her attention but, when a young man determined to make his mark on the world, he found her a tireless ally.

2 HIS FATHER Winston idolised Lord Randolph, but could never feel that it had been a mutual respect. Late in life, he wrote a story in which his father appeared to him in a dream, saying dismissively that he had hoped Winston might be a lawyer but he had not proved clever enough. Seeing his son's enthusiasm for playing with his vast collection of toy soldiers, Lord Randolph had directed him towards the army instead.

3 HIS NARROW ESCAPE The shrapnel that 'might have separated us for ever but is now a token of union' is a memento of one of Winston's numerous incidents cheating death. In 1915 Churchill fought for his men to be issued with the new life-saving Brodie helmet or 'tin hat' in the trenches, where shrapnel was causing carnage. In the meantime, he adopted a French helmet for his own forays into no-man's land.

4 HIS PAINTBOX It was painting that Churchill credited with rescuing him from the deep depression that struck him in 1915 after the disastrous Gallipoli campaign. Though his first foray into art was with his children's painting set, and he continued to use watercolours for sketching, his wife Clementine soon recognised that oil paints were better suited to his temperament and arranged the purchase of paints, brushes and canvases.

5 HIS CLUB Winston founded The Other Club, which met fortnightly at the Savoy, in 1911 with his great friend F. E. Smith (later Lord Birkenhead), and his last attendance was on 10th December 1964. The membership – by their invitation only – covered a wide spectrum of strongly held opinion. Churchill claimed to have contributed the rule: 'Nothing in the rules or intercourse of the Club shall interfere with the rancour or asperity of party politics.'

6 HIS DISPATCH BOX Ministers and Shadow Ministers traditionally speak in the Commons at the 'dispatch boxes' placed on the table between them. Both were destroyed on 10th May 1941 when a bomb fell on the Chamber. After the war, New Zealand donated new boxes for use in the rebuilt Chamber, and the battered box Churchill had made do with as Prime Minister was presented to him 'as a memento of an historic period'.

8 HIS GARTER ROBES

(replica) Elizabeth II invested Churchill as a Knight of the Order of the Garter in 1953. The insignia, including a gold collar, lay on the Union Jack covering his coffin at his funeral before being returned to the Queen. When, 40 years later, his daughter Mary was appointed a Lady Companion to the Order, she was touched when the Queen said that she had been given the collar worn by her father.

7 HIS HAIRBRUSH

Though he barely needed them by 1939, the newly appointed First Lord of the Admiralty was honoured to receive – along with George VI and the ship's captain – a pair of brushes made from salvaged timber from HMS *Exeter*, damaged in the first naval battle of the war in the estuary of the River Plate. While the cruiser was repaired, the badly damaged German *Admiral Graf Spee* was scuttled off the coast of Uruguay.

9 HIS BIRTHDAY GIFT

This leather cover contains a greeting for his 80th birthday in 1954, signed by all MPs (except for five who objected in principle!). The expected resignation did not follow, and a political cartoon by David Low showed a vigorous young Churchill confronting his elderly colleagues in 1984: 'Winston, who has grown progressively younger since his eightieth birthday, gives a half-promise that he will resign on reaching the age of fifteen.'

10 HIS ROSE

The Churchill Rose is a shrub rose introduced in 2011 to celebrate the 50th anniversary of Churchill College, Cambridge and now grows in the gardens at Chartwell. Churchill College, which received its Royal Charter in 1960, is itself 'the national and Commonwealth memorial to Sir Winston Churchill, Britain's great wartime Prime Minister – the embodiment of his vision for how higher education can benefit society in the modern age.'

Churchill: A Life in Politics

Winston Churchill remained a House of Commons man all his life. Over 64 years, there were barely 24 months when he was not a Member of Parliament – though he did not always serve in the same Party.

Constituencies

Oldham: 1st October 1900 to 12th January 1906

Manchester North West: 12th January 1906 to 24th April 1908

Dundee: 9th May 1908 to 15th November 1922

Epping: 29th October 1924 to 5th July 1945

Woodford: 5th July 1945 to 15th October 1964

Offices

Under-Secretary of State (Colonial Office) 1905–8

President of the Board of Trade 1908–10

Home Secretary 1910–11

First Lord of the Admiralty 1911–15

Minister of Munitions 1917–18

Secretary of State (War and Air) 1919–22

Chancellor of the Exchequer 1924–9

Prime Minister 1940–5

Prime Minister 1951–5

Father of the House of Commons 1959–64

Contributions

First recorded, 18th February 1901: 'Address in answer to His Majesty's Most Gracious Speech', Commons.

Last recorded, on 30 29,232

'At the bottom of all the tributes paid to democracy is the little man, walking into the little booth, with a little pencil, making a little cross on a little bit of paper ... No amount of rhetoric or voluminous discussion can possibly palliate the overwhelming importance of the point.'

WINSTON SPENCER CHURCHILL

PART ONE
1874–1905

CHAPTER 1

'Your loving son Winny'

If we were to glance up from Winston Churchill's desk in his study, we might imagine him transported from Chartwell to another, far grander house. For our view is filled with a painting of Blenheim Palace. Here he was born, and here his wife accepted his proposal of marriage. Just beyond its rolling grounds, in the churchyard at Bladon, where his parents are buried, Winston and Clementine, too, would rest when their time came.

A gift from the nation to John Churchill, 1st Duke of Marlborough, the house was reward for his decisive victory over Louis XIV in 1704 at the Battle of Blenheim. Winston – named after the 'Cavalier Colonel' father of the 1st Duke – began life in that palace, as the grandson of the 7th. Though, as son of a younger son, he was only ever for a very short period in line to inherit either house or title.

His father, charming and arrogant, was running with the racy set around the young Prince of Wales when, during Cowes Week 1873, at the age of 24, Lord Randolph Churchill met and fell in love with the 19-year-old American heiress Jeanette ('Jennie') Jerome. With her dark beauty and rumoured Iroquois blood, her cosmopolitan education and vivacious chic, Jennie epitomised the 'snap' and

OPPOSITE: Until the age of five, Winston wore his red hair in ringlets – echoing his Cavalier namesake. The first Winston Churchill had been named after his mother, Sarah Winston.

force of the 'Dollar Princesses' who would enrich the bloodlines and coffers of the British aristocracy over the coming decades. An American bride, she once wrote wryly, was assumed to be something between 'a Red Indian and a Gaiety Girl'. But this was a love match on both sides: Lord Randolph proposed and was accepted at their third meeting. Neither set of parents wholly approved but the following April, in Paris, the pair married.

His American grandfather was, Winston once remarked, 'very fierce. I'm the only tame one they've produced.' Leonard Jerome speculated in railroads and race tracks and, while his wife and daughters lived mostly in Paris, his mistress Jenny Lind, the 'Swedish nightingale', performed in the private opera house of his New York mansion (where, the newspapers gloated, separate ballroom fountains flowed with eau de cologne and champagne).

Lord Randolph had set his sights on becoming an MP, and was elected for Woodstock near Blenheim just before his marriage. Jennie took to her new life like a fish to water, venturing out into the streets to campaign for her husband in a way no Victorian lady was supposed to do. The American whirlwind took London society by storm, but was taken aback by the awe-inspiring but, to her eyes, uninviting – and icy cold – Blenheim. Where, during a winter shooting party, after a jolting carriage ride, Jennie went into premature labour.

Early on 30th November 1874, in the small, ground-floor bedroom of the family's chaplain, commandeered for the party as a ladies' cloakroom, her son was born. He was baptised in the family chapel Winston Leonard Spencer Churchill: Winston for the founder of the Churchill fortunes; Leonard for his American grandfather; his full surname Spencer Churchill reflecting a long-ago marriage with the wealthy Spencers of Althorp.

Winston did not see much of Blenheim in his earliest years, as the young family was effectively exiled to Dublin after a bitter row between Lord Randolph and

ABOVE: An admirer recalled Jennie: 'A diamond star in her hair, her favourite ornament – its lustre dimmed by the flashing glory of her eyes. More of the panther than of the woman in her looks.'
OPPOSITE: Elizabeth Everest, by contrast with his mother, was the warm, unglamorous heart of Winston's home, and the constant correspondent – and saviour – of his schooldays.

the Prince of Wales. The Duke of Marlborough was appointed Lord-Lieutenant of Ireland with instructions to take his son to Dublin with him.

It was in Ireland that Winston's beloved brother John ('Jack') was born – another premature birth. Lord Randolph's heir and spare were both looked after by the redoubtable Mrs Everest ('Woom' or 'Woomany'), from whom most of their direct motherly nurturing came and to whom Winston remained devoted for the rest of her life – and his. It is to Mrs Everest, more than anyone, that 'Winny' owed that warmth and generosity of spirit which, in later life, redeemed him to his friends for his more exasperating qualities. At Harrow, he defied schoolboy convention by inviting her to visit, parading proudly at Woomany's side along the High Street – even kissing her in full view of the other boys. It was, said a schoolfriend who went on to win the DSO, 'one of the bravest acts I have ever seen.'

Winston adored both of his parents too, responding particularly to the powerful attraction of his mother but, he wrote later, she was the Evening Star: 'I loved her dearly – but at a distance.' His father was even more remote: busy making his name in politics after returning to grace – and Westminster – when Winston was five. In later years, after one illuminating evening with his own son, Winston claimed it was more conversation than he'd had with his father in the whole course of his life.

Still, Winston took a keen interest in his father's career from a distance. Lord Randolph's 'Tory Democracy' aimed to capture the new working-class vote with progressive policies that often set him at odds with his own party. His preferred position was, it was remarked, looking down on the front benches of both sides.

Aged seven, Winston was detached from Mrs Everest and sent to a preparatory school, where the headmaster administered dreadful birchings for any infringement of the rules – and Winston infringed many rules. 'Very bad – a constant trouble to everybody,' came one report to his despairing parents.

A later schoolboy legend had it that he was beaten for stealing sugar from the pantry and kicked the headmaster's straw hat to pieces in revenge. By his own account, he 'offended' the masters at St George's, Ascot, aged nine, by devouring with delight the *Treasure Island* his father sent him, despite languishing at the bottom of the class: they viewed him as 'at once backward and precocious'. His salvation came during the next holidays: the family doctor wrote to Lord Randolph suggesting he transfer his son to the school his own boy attended – which did not practise corporal punishment. Churchill always chalked up this rescue to Mrs Everest's intervention, saying she saved him from being broken down completely: 'Can you imagine a child being *broken down*? I can never forget that school. It was horrible.'

'Can you imagine a child being broken down? *I can never forget that school. It was horrible.'*

In Brunswick Road, Hove, Winston's tasted the oft-vaunted 'happiest days of your life' schooldays of legend: half a century later he wrote, 'The impression of those years makes a pleasant picture in my mind.' In his first term, Miss Charlotte Thomson wrote to say Winston had been stabbed in the chest with a penknife. Jennie wrote to her husband, then in India, that Winston probably started it '& it ought to be a lesson to him'. He had, it transpired, been pulling the boy's ear. 'What adventures Winston does have,' replied Lord

Randolph. The blade had gone in a quarter of an inch: 'It is a great mercy he was no worse injured.'

The educative regime of Kate and Charlotte Thomson seems to have been less about moulding boys into shape than drawing out their natural talents and enthusiasms. Here Winston learned French, to love history and to memorise 'lots of Poetry' by heart. 'Above all' there was horse-riding and swimming. He never saw as much of his parents as he wanted and was desperately hurt that his father twice made a speech in nearby Brighton without coming to see him. But both parents hurried to his bedside in the wake of the pneumonia that, for a few days, was in serious danger of carrying him off. By the summer, recovered enough to return to school, Winston took a keen interest in the election that returned the newly named Conservative and Unionist Party to power – and elevated his father to Chancellor of the Exchequer.

At 37, Lord Randolph was spoken of as a future party leader, but in the run-up to Christmas 1886 he made the mistake of his career. Faced with opposition over cutting the Army and Navy budgets to pay for his social policies, he misjudged his own power and sent a resignation letter to the Prime Minister – which was accepted. It says something that Jennie only learned her husband was no longer Chancellor when she read it in *The Times*. At the pantomime in Brighton, Winston witnessed a sketch about his father and, when people hissed, he burst into tears, rounded on the man behind and said, 'Stop that row you snub-nosed radical!' His father was in Morocco when Jennie's letter reached him – and he arranged for Winston to be sent a gold sovereign.

Of his mother's many suitors, Winston was perhaps the most persistent: almost into adulthood, his letters to Jennie would sound the same pleading note as he begged for letters or visits. In 1887, three letters in one week cajoled her into getting the school to release him for London's Golden Jubilee celebrations – and

OPPOSITE: The Victorian vision of a serene and bountiful Empire – coloured pink. Burma (east of India) was added during Lord Randolph's time at the India Office.
ABOVE: *Vanity Fair* cartoons, drawn 20 years apart, poignantly capture Winston's schoolboy hope of emulating his father by becoming an MP.

'Buffalow [sic] Bill's Wild West Show and a play'. This last may have been Henry Irving's *Faust*: Bram Stoker, author of *Dracula* but then the manager of the Lyceum Theatre, recalled being introduced there to Winston, then 'about thirteen … with red hair and very red cheeks' by his father. Lord Randolph had patted Winston's shoulder, saying: 'He's not much yet, you know. But he's a good 'un. He's a good 'un!' (Though Jennie received another letter, on Winston's return to school, apologising for his behaviour while at home.)

Lord Randolph's Icarus-like career was now in free-fall. His behaviour became increasingly erratic; his condition believed, erroneously, to be syphilis. 'One could not grow up in my father's house,' Winston wrote later, 'and still less among his mother and sisters, without understanding that there had been a great political disaster.'

The Duchess of Marlborough had the boys to stay when Woomany fell ill while their parents were holidaying over Christmas and New Year with the Tsar and Tsarina of Russia. His grandmother described Winston, aged 13, in words that would have served him just as well at 30 – or indeed could have been carved upon his gravestone: 'Certainly a handful.' But she believed Harrow would sort him out.

Lord Randolph was disappointed by his son's performance at Harrow, however, and insisted on Winston being streamed into the 'army form' – a suitable slot for the undistinguished scholar he was proving to be. School over, he won, at third attempt, a cavalry cadetship (which required fewer marks than an infantry one but, as his angry father pointed out, more financial support for the horses).

At Sandhurst military academy Winston, finally, came into his own. After 15 months he passed out with honours. Even his father had noted he was 'much smartened up' at Sandhurst. It was the acknowledgement Winston always dreamed of – but then the following month, at the age of 45, Lord Randolph Churchill died.

Six months later, Mrs Everest fell ill with peritonitis and Winston rushed to her bedside. When the family had 'let go' their ageing nanny-turned-housekeeper, Winston wrote to his mother in a fury – and had started sharing some of his own inadequate allowance with his beloved 'Woomany'. Winston was 'one in ten thousand', Mrs Everest wrote gratefully to her 'dear dear Boy'. Now Winston sat with her through her final night. His warmest connection had been with Woomany; his father's death was hard because of their failure to connect. It was an end to his dreams of entering Parliament at his father's side. 'There remained for me only to pursue his aims and vindicate his memory.'

ABOVE: 'Certainly a handful' – the feisty young redhead that his family and schoolfriends knew looks boldly out of a recently discovered group photograph from his Harrow days.

CHAPTER 2

'Adventure for adventure's sake'

The death of his father left Winston 'the master of my fortunes,' he wrote. Whatever legacy Lord Randolph left his son, it included little cash, while his American grandfather had died pretty much cleaned out in 1891. The salary of a second lieutenant in the 4th Hussars paid perhaps a quarter of the expenses needed to maintain the lifestyle the rank demanded and, like his mother – 'still at 40 young, beautiful and fascinating' – Winston would always have expensive tastes.

His Army commission did however allow a generous five months' annual leave and Winston set out to make the most of it. Most young cavalry officers spent spare time fox hunting; his plans were at once more ambitious and more practical. Untested in battle, he sought 'a private rehearsal, a secluded trial trip, in order to make sure that the ordeal was one not unsuited to my temperament.'

He had his eye on the celebrity that had paid off in politics for his father and found his talent for words could take him into the line of fire. On the eve of his 21st birthday, a new war correspondent for *The Graphic* illustrated newspaper stood on the deck of the steamer *Olivette*, watching the outline of Cuba break against the Caribbean dawn: feeling, Winston wrote, like one of Long John Silver's pirate crew sighting Treasure Island for the first time.

He was there to report on a war of Empire. Not of Queen Victoria's British Empire – currently at its most powerful and secure across the globe – but a dying gasp of its oldest imperial rival Spain, beset by guerilla freedom fighters. His reports – naturally but, he later admitted, unfairly – reflected the views of the imperial forces to which he attached himself, earning him criticism on both sides of the Atlantic. Not for the last time, Winston Churchill had now found himself on the wrong side of history.

Still, seeking 'adventure for adventure's sake', it was in Cuba Winston first heard 'bullets strike flesh or whistle through the air' and felt the sheer exhilaration of

OPPOSITE: Winston, photographed in Aldershot in his 4th Queen's Own Hussars uniform. He celebrated his actual coming of age being shot at on a daredevil escapade.

knowing they hadn't struck him. In battle on his 21st birthday, a bullet whizzed by his head with barely a foot to spare, killing a horse behind him. The following day snipers attacked the gang of officers he took bathing in a local river.

On his return he reported back to the head of British military intelligence – who had privately briefed him beforehand – on the weapons on both sides. Technological innovation – what Winston would later call 'The Wizard War' – was an imperative of imperial sustainability and the British Empire would soon face guerillas of its own.

Churchill returned from Cuba with a supply of fine cigars, a respect for the restorative powers of the *siesta*, and a new profession. The next five years would see his role as army officer combined with writing commissions. To ensure he was posted where his talents might be best displayed, Jennie's connections were enlisted: 'She left no stone unturned, she left no cutlet uncooked,' he wrote. In vain. From late 1886, he was stuck in a quiet Indian posting to Bangalore. Though

ABOVE: Churchill acknowledged that the Cuban guerrillas had greater local support than the Spanish. He predicted, accurately, that the United States would soon get involved in this war.

impatient with the lack of conflict, it also impressed him. While his youthful fame and career would be built on what Kipling called 'the savage wars of peace', it was this peace – as he, at least, perceived it – that would reinforce Churchill's belief in Empire. As one of a few thousand British troops stationed in a region of millions of Indians, he wrote to his brother Jack: 'It is a proud reflection that all this vast expanse of fertile, populous country is ruled and administered by Englishmen. It is all the prouder when we reflect how complete and minute is the ruling – and how few are the rulers.'

Determined to profit from his boredom, he set about a programme of self-education, reading Darwin (having been inspired by a memorable lecture at Harrow), economist Adam Smith and Plato (in translation). He devoured history at the rate of 50 pages of Macaulay (12 volumes, courtesy of his mother) and 25 of Gibbon per day; ploughed through 27 volumes of *The Annual Register* for its detailed record of Parliamentary transactions and converted to an aggressive atheism under the influence of a book with the 'depressing conclusion that we simply go out like candles.' He converted back soon after when, under fire, he found he 'did not hesitate to ask for special protection' and was delighted to find it granted.

In a land where 'the deities of a hundred creeds were placed by respectful routine in the Imperial Pantheon,' spiritual matters were often discussed. Senior officers spoke of the beneficial effect of Christianity in controlling women and the lower orders but the general feeling amongst the younger men was that different religious rituals represented 'merely the same idea translated into different languages to suit different races and temperaments.'

'There was general agreement that if you tried your best to live an honourable life and did your duty and were faithful to friends and not unkind to the weak and poor, it did not matter much what you believed or disbelieved. All would come out right.'

In late 1897, Winston managed to attach himself for around six weeks to the Malakand Field Force policing the Afghan frontier, producing columns for an Indian paper and the *Daily Telegraph* (though, to his annoyance, *sans* byline). Winston quoted at the opening of his book recent words of Lord Salisbury at Guildhall: frontier wars were, the Prime Minister had said, 'but the surf that marks the edge and the advance of the wave of civilization.' But what might sound picturesque in the City of London was a bloody, dangerous business up close, and

'There was general agreement that if you tried your best to live an honourable life and did your duty and were faithful to friends and not unkind to the weak and poor, it did not matter much what you believed or disbelieved. All would come out right.'

BRITISH BENEVOLENCE.

"It is painful to be obliged to use force against the weak."—*Earl Granville in House of Lords.*

Winston witnessed brutalities from his own Indian troops that he had no power to prevent – or report. He felt 'rather a vulture', he confided to a friend, his only excuse being that he might himself have ended up 'carrion' himself.

To Jennie, he wrote of riding his conspicuous grey along the skirmish line while everyone else lay sensibly under cover: 'Foolish perhaps, but I play for high stakes and given an audience there is no act too daring or too noble.' These were *Boy's Own* adventures without innocence.

His lucrative book about his adventure was a great success: 'Everybody is reading it,' the Prince of Wales wrote to him. Returning to his Bangalore backwater, Winston resumed work on his first – and only – novel: a Ruritanian fantasy whose eponymous Icarus-figure hero Savrola ('vehement, high, and daring'), blazed his way towards a probable early grave.

> *'Foolish perhaps, but I play for high stakes and given an audience there is no act too daring or too noble.'*

'Hope you will take Churchill. Guarantee he won't write.' The cable to Herbert Kitchener, British Sirdar of the Egyptian Army, came from one of Jennie's London friends. Kitchener planned to recapture the Sudan and avenge the death of General Gordon more than a decade before.

Winston had mobilised his mother in his cause, while securing what the Army might call 'a roving commission' from the *Morning Post* (so much for the assurances to Kitchener). Buying a German Mauser pistol in London, Winston headed for Cairo, via a tramp steamer at Marseilles. Attached to the 21st Lancers, he travelled south to Omdurman where, on 2nd September 1898, he took part in history's last great victorious cavalry charge (though British machine guns against native rifles and spears did more to determine the battle's outcome, leaving half the opposing force killed, wounded or captured).

Of the 50,000 enemy 'Dervishes' he later wrote publicly with respect: 'The valour of their deed has been discounted by those who have told their tale.'

A letter to his cousin Sunny, now the 9th Duke of Marlborough, thanked him for his help with his and Jennie's tangled finances, and confided his disgust at Kitchener's brutality to the enemy wounded, together with indifference to their own, after the battle.

Winston was not squeamish, he told Sunny: he had 'seen more war than most boys my age – probably more than any,' but the acts of barbarity at Omdurman left

OPPOSITE: Churchill's lifelong belief in an essential moral purpose to Britain's Empire did not always find an echo across the Atlantic.

CHURCHILL and MAWDSLEY

FOR

OLDHAM

Printed and Published by G. Falkner & Sons, 170 Deansgate, Manchester

him 'sickened of human blood'. He would now try the fray of politics. But after a happy summer fighting – and only narrowly losing – a marginal seat in Oldham, he heard one last, *fin de siècle* call to adventure.

Churchill sailed for South Africa on 14th October 1899, two days after a second war broke out with its long-time Dutch Boer colonists, after clashes with recent British imperial expansion. Winston headed for Cape Town with 60 bottles of alcohol in his luggage, along with a dozen of Rose's Lime Juice – and his roving commission from the *Morning Post*. Plus – 'correspondent-status notwithstanding' – his Mauser, just in case.

He seized the chance to travel through fighting territory on an armoured train; on 15th November it was ambushed by Boers on horseback and part-derailed. Winston helped get the front half of the train moving again but, jumping down on the track to help men aboard, he found himself staring down the barrel of a Mauser rifle in the hands of a Boer sharpshooter – who he later came to believe was General Paul Botha himself. To his horror, he realised his own Mauser had been left on the train while helping the driver; he had no choice but to surrender. As the half-train steamed to safety, the miserable captives marched for two days, then a train took them to a school-turned-prison-camp 280 miles inside enemy territory.

His captors were not cruel, but to be a prisoner of war was both 'painful and humiliating,' he wrote. Winston's attempts to claim journalist status were rejected, as was his word not to serve against the Boers nor pass on intelligence if released; his father's name was 'better known than liked in the Transvaal' he discovered.

After 24 days of utter misery, Winston scaled the wall; with characteristic panache he whistled as he walked through town in his non-committal brown suit, pretending to know where he was going. He followed the railway line for two hours, boarded, then later jumped off, a goods train. Still some 200 miles from safety, after a day's wandering he had to risk seeking help. Incredibly – one of those happenings that made Winston bless his 'star' – the men who opened the first door he knocked on were English-born. One was from Oldham: everyone

OPPOSITE: Churchill's first attempt to get into Parliament, as a candidate in the two-seat constituency of Oldham, ended in defeat. But he saw it as useful practice.
BELOW: Capture and imprisonment as a Boer prisoner-of war was an experience that had a profound, long-lasting effect on Churchill (pictured far right).

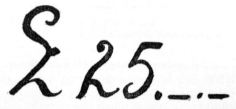

£25.—.—

(vijf en twintig pond stg.)
belooning uitgeloofd door
de sub-Commissie van Wijk V
voor den Specialen Constabel
dezer wijk, die den ontvluchte
Krijgsgevangene
Churchill
levend of dood te dezen kantoor
aflevert.—

Namens de sub-Comm.
Wijk V
OdodeHaas
Sec.

Translation.

£25

(Twenty-five Pounds stg.) REWARD is offered by the
Sub-Commission of the fifth division, on behalf of the Special Constable
of the said division, to anyone who brings the escaped prisoner of war

CHURCHILL,

dead or alive to this office.

For the Sub-Commission of the fifth division,
(Signed) LODK. de HAAS, Sec.

there would vote for Winston next time around, he was assured. They hid him,
well-provisioned, down a mineshaft, while Boer posters offered £25 for his
capture 'dead or alive'. After a week, he was smuggled into a wool truck headed for
Portuguese territory; arriving three days later, he sought out the British consulate.

Winston Churchill's capture had been widely reported and he arrived back in
Durban to a hero's welcome: a harbour decorated with flags; bands on the quays;

ABOVE: An escaped prisoner with a price on his head, Winston Churchill's story could have ended
almost before it had begun. But, as so often in his life, a lucky star seemed to save him.

himself borne aloft on the shoulders of the crowds. After which 'blaze of triumph' he rejoined the Army with a lieutenant's commission in the South African Light Horse, without even having to give up his press reporting. His 'victory' had been a welcome diversion from British defeats in a war that was shaking British Imperial confidence to the core.

As the war tide turned, Churchill had more adventures: climbing through the dark with a vital message at the Battle of Spion Kop; riding a bicycle through the Boer-occupied streets of Johannesburg to get another to General Roberts. He even had the delight of meeting Jennie, who arrived on a hospital ship funded in part by the American Ladies' Hospital Ship Society she headed (his brother Jack, shot through the ankle, was coincidentally one of its first officer patients).

Winston's *Morning Post* despatches now controversially urged a 'generous and forgiving policy' towards the Boers once the inevitable victory came – but his own eyes were turned towards home. In the 'Khaki Election' of 1900 he contested his seat as a hero and international celebrity. Ten weeks after returning to England he was Member of Parliament for Oldham.

How typically Winston then that, when the new Parliament met on 3rd December, he was sailing to New York for a lucrative lecture tour (until 1911, MPs received no wages, and he had a living to make). He stayed in New York with one of Jennie's friends; was introduced at his first lecture by Mark Twain. Things were done very differently here, he told brother Jack (now back in London). Paper dollar bills rather than gold sovereigns appalled him but he was impressed by New York firemen's rapid deployment down poles from their sleeping quarters: 'Mr Cockran got the Fire Commissioners to come with us and we alarmed four or five fire stations,' he wrote cheerily.

By the time Winston returned home on 10th February, Queen Victoria was dead, succeeded by Edward VII. It was a new era in other ways too. At 46, Jennie had remarried: George Cornwallis-West was 20 years her junior and barely a fortnight older than Winston himself. Arriving home, Winston sent her a letter enclosing a large cheque for one of her charities: the money was hers, he wrote: 'for I could never have earned it had you not transmitted to me the wit and energy which are necessary.' A few days later, on 18th February 1901, he went to Westminster to consummate his lifelong love affair with the House of Commons.

CHAPTER 3

'The new century of storm and change'

Winston Churchill entered the House of Commons very much his father's son. The 'kindness and patience' with which it heard his maiden speech must be, he said gracefully, down to 'a certain splendid memory'. Members with the longest memories may have reflected that the son was going to be as much trouble as the father. Defying the convention that maiden speeches avoid controversy, Winston, with his mother and several aunts watching through a grille from the Ladies' Gallery, declared: 'If I were a Boer I hope I should be fighting in the field', arguing for a magnanimous victory in a war with victory still a year away.

'Winston thinks with his mouth,' Liberal elder statesman Herbert Asquith once wrote disparagingly, but while his speeches were lengthy, many long nights went into their construction and memorising so he could deliver vivid fluency without notes and seemingly without effort. Forty-five minutes into one of them, the unthinkable happened: his prodigious memory failed him and, after agonising minutes, he was forced to sit down, covering his face with his hands in shame. After that he always brought notes: key points and pithy phrases on separate lines to prompt his memory.

Outside the House, Winston still had to make a living. Lectures and journalism brought an income but his father's literary executors were somewhat leery when he approached them about writing a biography of Lord Randolph. Who would control the content? Winston's attitude was robust: 'A syndicate may write an encyclopaedia, only a man can write a book.'

Socially, Winston was often in the company of his cousin the Duke, riding to hounds from Sunny's hunting box in Melton Mowbray, or relishing the Baroque

OPPOSITE: While he may have entered the House of Commons as his father's son, Winston was soon making a name for himself, a popular subject for parliamentary profiles.

splendour of Blenheim he adored: seven acres of Vanbrugh and Hawksmoor buildings and courtyards set within many more landscaped acres designed by Capability Brown. In Parliament, Winston found congenial company in the son of Prime Minister Lord Salisbury, the urbane Lord Hugh Cecil, and in the young and aristocratic 'Hughligans' around him: a group whose main object became 'to teach Winston not to talk too much,' according to one amused lady observer. Even after he diverged from Cecil's politics, Winston would retain his friendship – and the Hughligan method of wielding influence through eclectic dinner parties of the privileged and interesting.

In 'the new century of storm and change,' Churchill wrote, he 'drifted steadily to the left.' Mrs Everest had once scolded him when he spent 15 shillings in one week: 'Some families of six or seven people have to live upon twelve shillings a week. You squander it away & the more you have the more you want & spend.' While he would never curb his own spending, his reading now opened his eyes to this reality. And his sense of fair play demanded the rich ease poverty at the other end of the scale. The recent appearance on the political scene of the newly formed

ABOVE: Blenheim Palace, home of his cousin Sunny, played a regular home away from home to Winston in his youth and he delighted in its grandeur and grounds.
OPPOSITE: The Manchester homes of his constituents, cramped and smoky, appalled the radical young MP and, a Liberal at heart, he was determined to fight for something better.

Labour Party told him that an effective alternative to socialism was required – and he was beginning to doubt the Conservative Party was it.

In May 1901 Winston urged the Commons to 'peace, economy and reduction of armaments'. It was a conscious echo of the issue over which his father had resigned – curbing military spending to pay for social improvement. The British Empire was a 'commercial and maritime' affair, he declared: 'Standing armies, which abound on the European continent, are not indigenous to the British soil.' His speech earned cheers from the Opposition but marked 'a definite divergence of thought and sympathy from nearly all those who thronged the benches around me'.

The issue finally sundering Churchill's increasingly loose association with the Conservative Party was economic. Britain pursued the Free Trade policy of importing cheap food and raw materials from wherever they cost least, and selling the goods manufactured in the 'Workshop of the World' to whoever would pay the best price. But the Workshop now had competition. There had been a Second Industrial Revolution: a thing of telephones, bicycles, typewriters, motor cars and aeroplanes. And these were just as likely to be made in France as Britain. Or in Germany, Italy, America, even Japan. Meanwhile raw materials from other Empires' colonies competed with Britain's. A big new idea – British Imperial Preference Tariffs – would put up trade barriers to protect Empire goods.

Churchill was appalled at this revival of the 'quack remedies' of Protectionism. In spring 1903 he wrote to new Prime Minister Arthur Balfour: 'I am utterly opposed to anything which will alter the Free Trade nature of this country; & I consider such an issue superior in importance to any other now before us.'

If the party moved in that direction, he warned, 'I must reconsider my position in politics.' That autumn he wrote – though not to Balfour – 'I am an English Liberal. I hate the Tory party, their men, their words and their methods.'

On 29th March 1904, the Prime Minister walked out, followed by his ministers and MPs, as Churchill spoke. Winston sat down to Opposition cheers but it was a dreadful experience. Coincidentally or otherwise, it was three weeks later, speaking in favour of trade union rights, that he suffered his paralysing memory loss.

He also wrote an open letter against Balfour's policy towards the Jews fleeing antisemitic pogroms in the Russian Empire. While the Aliens Bill didn't mention

'I am an English Liberal. I hate the Tory party, their men, their words and their methods.'

them by name, it aimed to refuse refuge whenever and however possible. Winston condemned it as an 'appeal to insular prejudice against foreigners, to racial prejudice against Jews, and to labour prejudice against competition,' and praised 'the old tolerant and generous practice of free entry and asylum to which this country has so long adhered and from which it has so greatly gained.'

On 31st May, the day the letter was published in the *Manchester Guardian*, Winston finally 'crossed the floor' of the House of Commons, taking his seat on the Liberal benches beside equally radical Welshman David Lloyd George. (His cousins Ivor and Freddie Guest crossed too.) Churchill was now seen as a class traitor: he was blackballed at Hurlingham (which distressed him, since he loved polo) and had to resign from the Carlton Club. Jennie, still moving in royal

circles, found the situation socially awkward. Nonetheless, she was at Winston's side at a ball soon afterwards when he asked her to introduce him to a pretty young debutante. Clementine Hozier was the daughter of one of Jennie's old friends so nothing was easier – except that Winston found himself, uniquely, tongue-tied. With nothing to say, he watched Clementine disappear, rescued from the awkwardness by a friend.

He had been romantically involved before. At 16, Winston wrote of 'making an impression on the pretty Miss Weaslet,' to his mother. In India, he had paid his attentions to Pamela Plowden, beautiful daughter of the Resident of

Hyderabad; his name had also been linked to shipping heiress Muriel Wilson and to Helen Botha, daughter of the Boer leader; he is even said to have proposed to American actress Ethel Barrymore. Asquith's young daughter Violet probably had a crush on him but, though they were good friends, Winston's attention focused more on her politics than her person.

Churchill knew he could not win in his old seat in the general election of January 1906 but nearby Manchester North West, dominated by the textile trade, was committed to Free Trade. The previous summer he had set up his standard here as champion of what he would call 'the left-out millions', condemning Imperial Tariffs as: 'sentiment by the bucketful, patriotism by the imperial pint … dear food for the million, cheap labour for the millionaire.' Returning to fight the election, he toured the slums. 'Imagine living in these streets,' he said, 'Never seeing anything beautiful – never eating anything savoury – *never saying anything clever*!'

Manchester was also heartland of the Women's Social and Political Union (soon dubbed 'suffragettes' by the *Daily Mail*), a splinter group of the suffragist movement whose 'deeds not words' campaign aimed to force sympathetic Liberals to declare for Votes for Women. At the first meeting of Churchill's campaign, in Manchester's Free Trade Hall with Sir Edward Grey in attendance, Annie Kenney asked for Churchill's position on the issue and, when he ignored her, she and Christabel Pankhurst chanted, 'The question, the question, answer the question.' Hustled out, they waited to address people as they left but were arrested and fined. They refused to pay and were sentenced to a few days in prison. Churchill's offer to pay the fines was refused by the prison governor and both women emerged as heroines to their own packed meeting in the Free Trade Hall – a new and powerful campaign was born.

As it increased in vehemence, Churchill told hecklers: 'The only time I have voted in the House of Commons on this question I have voted in favour of women's suffrage, but having regard of the perpetual disturbance of public meetings in this election, I utterly decline to pledge myself.'

The election produced a Liberal landslide that gave new Prime Minister Sir Henry Campbell-Bannerman a more than 240-seat majority. It was an epoch-making mandate for what became one of the most radical reforming governments in British history – and Winston Churchill would be part of it.

OPPOSITE: Clementine Hozier was an independent-minded young woman and a dedicated Liberal – as she would remain, irrespective of Winston's changing political allegiance.

PART TWO
1906–18

CHAPTER 4

'Peaceful co-operation'

Churchill made around 700 speeches, long and short, in his first year in his new job as Under-Secretary for the Colonies (a role formerly filled by his cousin Sunny for the Tories). Since the Minister was in the House of Lords, topics on which Winston spoke in the House of Commons or answered questions in 1906 included: slave selling in British Columbia and motor traction in Nigeria; gun-running in Zululand and coal taxes in Brunei; sleeping sickness in Uganda and the New Zealand butter industry; Ceylon pearl fisheries and the preservation of African fauna; Hindoos [sic] in British Columbia and Christian missionaries in Tristan de Cunha; gambling in the Malay States and Irish emigration to Canada; religious processions in Malta and opium revenue collection; gold output in the Transvaal and silver coinage in Australia; the Kowloon to Canton railway and lions on the loose in Chiromo.

However, all Winston's undeniable hard work and best intentions would earn him few plaudits, especially from history. To be progressive – for an Imperialist – is a flower that has long ago lost its bloom. One case in point arose on only the third day of the new Parliament. The South African indenture system for Chinese miners, which the Liberals had campaigned against, was to be abolished. Churchill

OPPOSITE: The showman in Churchill relished every bit of the democratic process – as much the appeal to voters at election time as persuading his fellow MPs in the House.

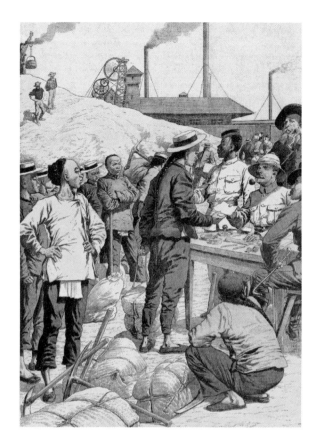

was persuaded, very reluctantly, that it could only end slowly or it would crash the local economy, and it now fell to him to speak against an Opposition amendment regretting ministers had 'brought the reputation of this country into contempt' by calling it 'slavery'.

The Liberals, Churchill responded, were 'doing the very best we can do to undo the harm which has been done' from this 'evil inheritance'. The delay was not to benefit the mine owners, who would still have millions, he said scornfully. Rather, there was a duty to protect the 'thousands of small people' from 'the harsh and unexpected pinch of poverty and suffering' of a slump.

History would forget all these words, however. What would echo down the ages was a single shudderingly memorable phrase: the system could not, Churchill said, 'be classified as slavery in the extreme acceptance of the word without some risk of terminological inexactitude.'

Churchill's huge responsibilities at the Colonial Office, watching over the lives of 100 million people, were, of course, dwarfed by those at the India Office, where his father had watched over twice as many. Winston's biography of Lord Randolph had just been published to excellent reviews. As Secretary of State there, his father had been judged, by his chief civil servant, an excellent head of a great department. Winston said it was incumbent on Westminster to supply India with 'wise, experienced and courageous' government. Democracy didn't come into it: 'In India it is not as in England,' Winston wrote. 'In India there is no public opinion to speak of, no powerful press, and hardly any trammels upon Government of any sort or kind.'

ABOVE: Indentured Chinese workers in South Africa suffered conditions which, if not actual slavery, were very harsh. The practice gradually ended, with workers deported back to China.
OPPOSITE: London-trained Mohandas K. Gandhi, practising law in South Africa, was outraged by a new local ordinance that treated Indians as second-class citizens.

Later that year, Churchill agreed to meet with a Hindu barrister from South Africa, five years older than him, who would destroy that illusion within a generation.

Schoolboy Winston could have bumped into barrister Mohandas K. Gandhi in London during Gandhi's Inns of Court studies – the training Lord Randolph thought beyond his son's intelligence. Or in the Boer War: Churchill wrote of Spion Kop's trenches, 'choked with dead and wounded, [who] … splinters and fragments of the shells had torn and mutilated'; Gandhi was there as a volunteer stretcher-bearer with the Natal Indian Ambulance Corps. However, in 1906, Churchill was smoothing the passage of the Boer and British colonies into a single Union of South Africa. And Gandhi and a Muslim colleague had just arrived from there, coming 6,000 miles to protest against an Ordinance under which every Asian man, woman and child over eight must be registered and fingerprinted, 'as if they were a barbarous race', said Gandhi. After a friendly interview, Churchill announced to the Commons the Ordinance would not go through. However, he knew that it would pass a few months later – but under a new, local legislature. The Government was in 'a wholly indefensible position,' Churchill's departmental memo had explained, long before the meeting took place: 'The new … Parliament may shoulder the burden. Why should we?'

This deft deflection would have consequences. Gandhi seems not to have held the betrayal against Churchill personally, but it showed the limits of polite lobbying. Barely a year later, Gandhi was in a South African prison for his campaign of passive resistance that he would later take home to India, where it would change the destiny of the British Empire.

Speaking in the Commons on 15th July 1907, Churchill said Free Traders like himself:

'… cherish the British Empire because it represents more than any similar organisation has ever represented, the peaceful co-operation of all sorts of men in all sorts of countries … a model of what we hope the world, the whole world will some day become.'

In the autumn recess, he packed his suitcase with books about politics, saying 'I'm going to see what the Socialist case really is,' and set sail for the beautiful East African Protectorate (including present-day Kenya). His published observations are a mixture of the worst prejudices of his age with some sharp insights into how far some would-be colonists fell below his Imperial ideal.

He was sceptical of their declared wish to make this 'a white man's country' since 'the European has neither the wish nor the power to constitute a white proletariat … Room is left only for the capitalist *pure and simple* – if one may so describe him.' What of the native population, he asked: 'It is, after all, their Africa.' They must be made to work, he was told.

'"For whom?" we innocently ask. "For us of course," is the ready answer; "what do you think we meant?" And here we run into another herd of rhinoceros questions – awkward, thick-skinned, and horned, with a short sight, an evil temper, and a tendency to rush blindly up wind upon any alarm.'

He also found colonists 'shrieking vigorously' against 'educated Indians'. A long-established community in the region who, Churchill argued, 'may point to as many generations of useful industry on the coast and inland as the white settlers … Is it possible for any Government with a scrap of respect for honest dealing between man and man, to embark upon a policy of deliberately squeezing out the native of India from regions in which he has established himself under every security of public faith?' It was, he said, the riddle of the Sphinx. But, he wrote hopefully: 'There is plenty of room for all. Why cannot we settle it fairly?'

In April 1908 ill health forced Campbell-Bannerman to resign and Herbert Asquith became Prime Minister. Churchill thought he was now quite ready to move up to Colonial Secretary: 'I know military & Colonial things.' But it was as President of the Board of Trade that he became, at 33, the youngest Cabinet member in 40 years. Merchant shipping, transport, power, factories, companies and labour conditions now all came under his purview. He was flying high: a letter from Asquith's wife told him no aim should be too high: 'Let us say for short the P. Minister wd be my ambition.'

He had also met Clementine Hozier again. It was at a dinner party given by one of the influential society ladies who had pulled strings on his behalf when he was looking for high-profile postings. Clementine was her great-niece.

This time they spoke, and Winston asked Jennie to invite Clementine to spend a day – it turned out to be the same weekend that he was appointed a Minister. She

was on the verge of going abroad for some weeks; Winston had an election campaign to plan – at that time ministers needed to be re-elected. Still, he took time out from 'the storm' that week to write to her, saying what a pleasure it had been to talk with a girl possessed of 'so much intellectual quality & such strong reserves of noble sentiment.'

Clementine did not then, it was clear, take after her mother. Whether she took after her father was more difficult to say, since Blanche (or 'Natty') Ogilvy had taken a stream of lovers after her marriage of convenience to the much older Sir Henry Hozier. One candidate for Clemmie's father was Bertie Mitford (her mother's brother-in-law); another the dashing Captain 'Bay' Middleton, who had also squired Empress Elizabeth of Austria. Clementine's mother and Winston's led equally colourful lives. But Clemmie's rebellion against her erratic, hard-drinking, heavy-spending mother was to pursue a very different course.

The storm Winston had mentioned now blew him briefly out of Parliament. Winston was, unexpectedly, defeated in his Manchester by-election. (The Tory joke around Westminster was 'What use is a W.C. without a seat?') Only a month later, in May, however, he won a safe seat in Dundee.

ABOVE: Midlands WSPU organiser Gladys Keevil campaigning against Churchill in Manchester North in 1908. Suffrage campaigners would make him a particular target.

In August his brother Jack, now a stockbroker, married Lady Gwendoline Bertie, daughter of the Earl of Abingdon. The night before the wedding, Winston was staying in a mansion rented by Freddie Guest when it caught fire. He was delighted when the news story about his daring rescue drew an alarmed telegram from Clementine. He invited her to Blenheim, and when he asked her on the day she arrived whether she would walk with him next day after breakfast, it was clear a proposal was on its way. But perhaps Winston the Intrepid was, for once, scared. He overslept, and had to be routed out of bed by Sunny. As they sheltered from sudden rain in Blenheim's Temple of Diana folly, Winston proposed and 'Clemmie' accepted, agreeing to marry in a month's time – so that the honeymoon could be over before the end of Parliament's summer recess.

Violet Asquith comforted herself that Winston's wife 'could never be more to him than an ornamental sideboard as I have often said & she is unexacting enough not to mind not being more. Whether he will ultimately mind her being as stupid as an *owl* I don't know ...'

This was unfair. Despite the businesslike start to their marriage, this became a notably strong and enduring love story and a true partnership. The couple's almost-constant correspondence when apart offers ample evidence that Winston was deeply devoted to Clemmie and more than grateful for her Loyal Opposition. Her influence 'when guiding & not contrary' he wrote in one letter, was of the utmost use. The supportive and – apparently – yielding Clementine was someone from whom even Winston could accept guidance. Later in life Violet Asquith would concede that Clementine had proved 'a better natural Liberal than Winston.'

Their wedding on 12th September, at the Parliamentary church of St Margaret's Westminster, was a great society event. Lord Hugh Cecil was best man; Lloyd George, a witness, signed the register, talking politics all the while.

Looking back, 20 years later, Winston ended a volume of autobiography with the words: 'I married and lived happily ever afterwards.' It was almost true, despite their very different natures: Clemmie kept regular hours and worried about money, and disapproved of Winston's drinking, gambling and his more raffish friends. Bishop Welldon said at their wedding: 'There must be in the statesman's life many times when he depends upon the love, the insight, the penetrating sympathy and devotion of his wife.' Clementine would often find the role a challenging one, but Winston would acknowledge it was his wife who made 'my life & any work I have done possible.'

OPPOSITE: *Tatler's* coverage of Winston and Clementine's marriage – 'the wedding of the year' – reflected his position as a politician for whom great things were predicted.

CHURCHILL—HOZIER: THE WEDDING OF THE YEAR.

Mr. Winston Churchill and his best man, Lord Hugh Cecil, arriving at the church door

The bride arriving at St. Margaret's. On the left is her brother, Sub-Lieutenant Hozier, R.N.

Lady Sarah Wilson leaving Lady St. Helier's house after the reception

Four of the bridesmaids—Miss Madeleine Whyte, Miss Claire Frewen, the Hon. Venetia Stanley, Miss Horatia Seymour

The bride and bridegroom leaving for their honeymoon. Miss Nellie Hozier and Lady Blanche Hozier, mother of the bride, are seen on the right

Mrs. George Cornwallis-West, mother of the bridegroom

'What was notable,' wrote John 'Jock' Colville, who later became Winston's secretary and friend, 'was the way in which their qualities and defects complemented and cancelled each other … What he lacked, she provided.' From first to last she would put him first so consistently that, she later admitted to one of her daughters, she often had little left over to give the rest of them. Winston, for his part, was determined to have a much closer relationship with his children than his parents had built with him. The 'kittens', as he called them, came quickly: Diana in 1909; Randolph in 1911; Sarah in 1914. Clementine and Winston became to each other 'Cat' and 'Pug' (or 'Pig'), and visitors in later years would be taken aback by the family's habit of greeting each other with animal noises.

In his new job at the Board of Trade, his first task on his return from honeymoon was ending a series of dock strikes through arbitration. But Churchill had bigger plans. He wanted to give the British people social security.

Britain had 'an immense amount of voluntary private machinery in the shape of friendly and benefit societies, trade unions & the like' he wrote to one of his civil servants, asking for facts and figures on 4th January 1908 while he was still at the Colonial Office. Germany already had a state system, which scored less well in 'flexibility, in spontaneity, & possibly even in economy' but had one 'enormous advantage. It catches everybody.'

 In Britain, he wrote, those 'not found on any of those innumerable lists go smashing down on the pavement. It is this very class, the residue, the rearguard, call it what you will … who have neither the character nor the resources to make provision for themselves, who require the aid of the State.'

Now, he sat up all night writing out for Asquith his programme of social organisation: 'Dimly across gulf of ignorance I see the outline of a policy which I call the Minimum Standard.' He was bursting with ideas: unemployment insurance, disability insurance, compulsory training from 14 to 18 – 'the exploitation of Boy Labour must be absolutely stopped' – jobs in public works rather than poor relief, lifelong state employment for soldiers returning from the colonies, the de-casualisation of work through labour exchanges offering secure jobs and nationalising the railways. Not everything in Winston's plans made it to the Statute Book, but those things that did helped to lay the foundations of the welfare state, including the first old-age pensions (a move on which the shade of Mrs Everest in her final years might have smiled).

In April 1909, Chancellor Lloyd George presented the Liberals' 'People's Budget' explaining all this was to be paid for by raising unearned income tax

THE BUDGET LEAGUE.

THE TAX PAYER | THE TAX DODGER

30/- A WEEK | £20,000 A YEAR.

TAX THE LOAFER - NOT THE LOAF

from 12 pence in the pound (five per cent) to 14, with a 'super-tax' on the very rich. Also by raising death duties, taxes on alcohol, tobacco and the relatively new luxury of petrol, and by a land duty that would hit the owners of aristocratic estates. This was the first-ever overtly redistributive budget and cheerful class traitor Churchill was unsympathetic to dukes and duchesses 'howling and whining because they are asked to pay their share'. He recruited social worker William Beveridge (of whom history would hear further) to his staff and was in close touch with Fabian socialists Sidney and Beatrice Webb, who welcomed his 'definitely casting in his lot with constructive state action'.

In September 1909, Edward VII's nephew, Kaiser Wilhelm II, invited Churchill to watch the German Army on manoeuvres. Winston admired the German social security system. He liked its small neat farms, not walled off by ducal acres. But the disciplined, goose-stepping efficiency of the Kaiser's powerful standing army was a 'terrible engine,' he wrote to Clemmie. 'Much as war attracts me & fascinates my mind with its tremendous situations, I feel more deeply every year … what vile & wicked folly & barbarism it all is.'

ABOVE: Winston set up the Budget League to defend the Liberal budget from House of Lords opposition. This campaign postcard shows he was prepared to savage his own class.

CHAPTER 5

'The world is gone mad'

Churchill's trip to Germany meant missing his first wedding anniversary:
'A year ago today my lovely white pussy-cat came to me,' he wrote in his letter
home. 'My precious & beloved Clemmie my earnest desire is to enter still more
completely into your dear heart & nature & to curl myself up in your darling arms.
I feel so safe with you.'

Though safe at home, he was about to sail into dangerous political waters. In
January 1910 Asquith moved him from the Board of Trade to become the youngest
Home Secretary in almost a century. Though it was a huge step up, Churchill now
had the job of maintaining law and order in turbulent – some thought revolutionary
– times, and his reactions to their challenges would haunt him through his career.

His job switch came after the general election Asquith called when the House
of Lords rejected the People's Budget. The Liberals were returned to office – and
Churchill circulated a radical Cabinet memorandum calling for the House of Lords to
be abolished altogether. But his party's massive majority had now been reduced to just
two seats; what has been called 'The Strange Death of Liberal England' had begun.

Churchill began well. He continued to help with some of the reforms he had
begun at the Board of Trade. Measures included raising the minimum age of
employment in mines from 13 to 14 years old; winning a statutory meal break for
shopworkers (and trying but failing to limit the working week to 60 hours). He
also has a right to share credit with Lloyd George for the National Insurance Act.

His progressive programme for the Home Office, too, was radical, with
empathy for a section of the community with few friends. Criminals – or those
too-quickly judged to be criminals – now became his focus. He pointed out
that working-class boys were often jailed for offences written off as high jinks in
Oxbridge students, and introduced various measures to keep the young out of

OPPOSITE: Winston with his irrepressible mother Jennie, now Mrs Cornwallis-West, in the summer of
1912. The family resemblance is striking.

EN L'AN 2000

prison where possible. He once blocked a by-law to criminalise roller-skating on the pavement, explaining, 'I am very reluctant to increase the number of occasions when the children of the poorer classes may be brought into the police court and rendered liable to imprisonment.' Challenged that people could be killed by roller-skaters, he responded to Viscount Castlereagh: 'If we had proceeded on the principle that no person may be killed by such a pastime, the Noble Lord would ride more rarely than he does in motor cars.'

'If we had proceeded on the principle that no person may be killed by such a pastime, the Noble Lord would ride more rarely than he does in motor cars.'

Influenced by campaigners like playwright John Galsworthy, Churchill limited the use of solitary confinement and, for the first time, created a distinction for political prisoners, subject to a less harsh regime. Other measures helped prisoners on their release, while the idea of 'time to pay' for fines led to huge reductions in the numbers going to prison in the first place. Some reforms reflected his own experience as a prisoner. He told Violet Asquith that prisoners must have books: 'that's what I missed most' – apart, he said, from a means of escape: 'and I suppose I mustn't give them *that*'. Concerts and lectures, too, aimed to recognise and redeem the humanity in those the law must punish.

ABOVE: The super-modern 'Twentieth Century' opened up all sorts of possibilities for 'the year 2000' – like electric roller-skates. Churchill defended the (unpowered) craze in Parliament.

However, you cannot to this day, say 'Winston Churchill' in Wales and not expect to hear the word 'Tonypandy' in response. Though the story of Churchill deliberately sending soldiers to shoot miners is untrue, the more complex reality reflected the times.

In early November 1910, during a Welsh coal strike, pickets and police came to blows. When the local chief constable asked the War Office to send troops, Churchill asked the Army to be held back, 20 miles away in Cardiff, as a last resort. Meanwhile he sent several hundred Metropolitan Police reinforcements into the village of Tonypandy, including some 70 mounted officers. He expressly assured one editor that press reports about his intentions towards the miners were overblown:

> My dear Gardiner, give no credence to such rubbish.
> I do not anticipate any shooting & have taken some responsibility to that end – which Liberal newspapers should recognise/ Yours vy trly/ WS Churchill

A local magistrate, however, summoned the Army from Cardiff; there was a sustained window smashing and more Army patrols. In clashes, at least 500 citizens and over 70 police were injured. One man died, allegedly from a blow from a police truncheon. Huge peaceful demonstrations, held under the eye of police and soldiers, supported the 13 miners sent to trial.

For that was not the end of it. On 22nd November, strikers were forced down off the hillside by troops with fixed bayonets and forced to disperse by baton charges from the police. The local paper reported that Tonypandy's women 'displayed a total disregard of personal danger which was as admirable as it was foolhardy.' These 'Amazons of the coalfield' showered the police with boiling water from upstairs windows, with one London policeman receiving 'a piece of bedroom ware' to the head.

In the same month, Parliament Square in Westminster saw six hours of street fighting and over a hundred arrests, as women demonstrated for their promised Bill on women's suffrage to be given Parliamentary time. Earlier that year, as an MP, Churchill had presented a petition to Parliament on behalf of 5,000 Dundee voters (a quarter of his electorate) in favour of extending the franchise to women 'on the same terms as men'. But, as Home Secretary, he refused to institute an enquiry into allegations of police brutality on 'Black Friday', as it came to be known. Four days later a, 'torrent of indignant women' poured into Downing Street and the Prime Minister's windows were broken. Churchill was present and ordered the police to clear the women away; later that day, his own windows were broken.

A Suffragette in Prison.

The long dark night is almost gone,
And freedom's morn is drawing near :
From prison cell she sees the dawn
Of woman's liberty appear.

'I hope you will not be very angry with me for having answered the suffragettes sternly,' he had written to Clemmie the year before, 'I shall never try to crush your convictions … I must claim an equal liberty for myself. I have told them I cannot help them while the present tactics are continued.' Winston supported his wife's belief that women were entitled to the vote: he was reported as saying in a Dundee paper, 'The sex disqualification was not a true or logical disqualification.' Privately, he advocated a referendum to settle the matter. But neither he nor Clementine were happy with the turn the campaign was taking.

Suffragettes arriving at his meeting 'were much pelted with mud by angry ploughmen,' he wrote to Clemmie. She replied 'I am glad you were not interrupted & that the suffragettes were foiled.' She would always put him first: when a woman with a whip attacked Winston at a railway station, trying to force him off the platform into the path of an oncoming train, it was Clementine who, as the men around him stood frozen in shock, leapt over a pile of luggage to pull him to safety.

Churchill warned Asquith that unless the suffrage issue was dealt with, his Government might 'perish like Sisera at a woman's hand' (the Biblical heroine Jael had righteously hammered a tent peg into his head). The Government's reputation certainly perished, with its treatment of suffragettes remembered long after its People's Budget was consigned to the history books.

Another incident that added to Churchill's notoriety and bellicose reputation was the 'Siege of Sidney Street' in January 1911, which followed the murder of three policemen as they tried to stop a robbery by Latvian immigrants. With suspects cornered in an East End flat, Churchill authorised deployment of Scots Guards from the Tower of London as well as police marksmen. He also turned up in person, and was caught in press photographs and a Pathé newsreel. 'Who let them in?' bystanders shouted at the Home Secretary; colleagues derided him for grandstanding.

Years later, Churchill told his daughter Diana that it was as Home Secretary that he first suffered from depression. He now had the final word on death sentences. The first, after only a few days in the job, was of a man who had slit the throat of a three-year-old child then tried to commit suicide, saying he 'had been so depressed he didn't know what he was doing'. After signing his first death warrant on

OPPOSITE: This prophetic postcard was proved right. The ever more radical suffragette campaign was one of the greatest challenges Churchill faced while Home Secretary.

LEFT: When Churchill (in top hat at front) made a personal appearance at the Siege of Sidney Street, he was caught on camera and on film, adding to his notoriety.

21st February 1910, Winston sat brooding through a dinner party before turning to an older woman friend next to him and saying, 'After all, we make too much of death,' before pouring out how much the facts of the case weighed on him.

In July 1911 Winston wrote to Clementine about a German doctor who cured his cousin's wife of depression: 'I think this man might be useful to me – if my black dog returns. He seems quite away from me now – it is such a relief. All the colours come back into the picture.' Forty years later, he would call the Home Office the department he had been happiest to leave. It came as a huge relief when Asquith reshuffled his Cabinet in October 1911, swapping Churchill at the Home Office with Reginald McKenna at the Admiralty.

Churchill was now First Lord of the Admiralty. Over the previous seven years the Navy had gone through a massive modernisation. 'Jacky' Fisher, the First Sea Lord (professional head of all naval services), had encouraged British use of the innovative oil-driven submarine, and HMS *Dreadnought*, launched in 1906, had been a step-change in battleships, a steam turbine-driven vessel with 'all big gun' armaments. Fisher had recently retired, aged 70, but now kept up a lively correspondence with Churchill that undermined his relationships with his actual First Sea Lords.

Ruling the waves was for Britain no longer just a matter of pride, but of survival. Britain imported around 50 per cent of its meat and dairy produce and almost 80 per cent of its wheat and flour. It could fall to siege and starvation just like any medieval city. And as an arms race to build their own dreadnoughts gripped the world's great powers, Churchill wrote to the new King George V: 'The world is armed as it was never armed before.' In 1913, his attempt to introduce a 'naval holiday' – a year's pause in building warships on all sides – failed to halt the escalation.

Churchill did not believe in the 'theory of inevitable wars,' he wrote. But in peacetime, preparation was key. With much encouragement from Jacky Fisher, he took the fateful decision to switch the Royal Navy from coal to oil. This meant a speed advantage over Germany's coal-fired vessels but also changed global geopolitics forever. The oilfields that had just been discovered in the Persian Gulf were now crucial to Britain's own defence and supply lines. Churchill persuaded the Government to buy a controlling state in the Anglo-Persian Oil Company to guarantee supplies.

An early convert to the military potential of aircraft, Churchill had kept in touch with science-fiction writer H.G. Wells since their first meeting in 1902, and he understood what the reality of Wells's 1908 fictional *The War in the Air* could mean. Churchill set up an 'Air Department of the Admiralty' which explored

possibilities beyond the Army's Royal Flying Corps' reconnaissance planes. He also took flying lessons himself, undeterred by near misses and the deaths of fellow pilots. He was on the verge of taking his pilot's certificate when Clementine's pleas and those of his colleagues finally grounded him.

••• ———— •••

On 28th June 1914, Archduke Franz Ferdinand, heir to the Habsburg throne of Austro-Hungary, was shot and killed with his wife Sophie by a Serbian nationalist. The Emperor sent an ultimatum to Serbia and Russia, who he accused of fostering nationalists to bring down his empire, and the heavily armed German Empire backed him. The following month Churchill ordered a test mobilisation of the Fleet off Spithead – and the ships did not disperse when it ended, but remained battle-ready. The First Fleet was despatched to take up station in the North Sea, while the Second Fleet assembled at Portland.

On 28th July he wrote to Clementine (as he still did every day, when they were apart). 'My darling one & beautiful, Everything tends towards catastrophe and collapse. I am interested, geared up & happy. Is it not horrible to be built like that?' He would do his best for peace, and he profoundly understood her (presumably more pacific) views, 'But the world is gone mad – & we must look after ourselves – & our friends.'

ABOVE: A Puck cartoon shows Churchill's proposal of a 'naval holiday' in 1913, to de-escalate the arms race, being met with horror by other nations. He later argued it might have helped avert the Great War.

He Answered His

Country's Call

EARL KITCHENER

FIELD-MARSHAL SIR JOHN FRENCH

ADMIRAL SIR J. JELLICOE

RT. HON. WINSTON CHURCHILL

CHAPTER 6

'I should like the truth to be known'

Precisely how an assassination a thousand miles away led Britain to go to war on behalf of 'plucky little Belgium' is a conundrum that has filled libraries. Some point to the click-clack operations of the machinery of alliances, 'ententes' and guarantees; some talk of the underlying economic rivalries between powerful nations; even of the first war for oil – the Kaiser was building a railway from Berlin to Baghdad. Old grudges and new ambitions – and a failure of the diplomacy that had kept Britain out of European wars for half a century – finally came down to a 'scrap of paper'.

The Kaiser's war plans were predicated on a swift knock-out victory over France – this would allow him to take on the Russian Empire without having to watch his back. When, to circumvent French defences, his troops marched through Belgium, he was shocked to find it brought the Empire of his cousin George V into the war against him.

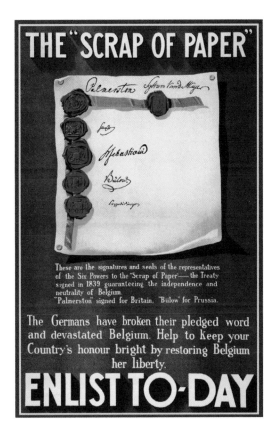

THE "SCRAP OF PAPER"

These are the signatures and seals of the representatives of the Six Powers to the "Scrap of Paper"— the Treaty signed in 1839 guaranteeing the independence and neutrality of Belgium. "Palmerston" signed for Britain, "Bülow" for Prussia.

The Germans have broken their pledged word and devastated Belgium. Help to keep your Country's honour bright by restoring Belgium her liberty.

ENLIST TO-DAY

OPPOSITE: The photograph of Sidney Howard James, killed in action in 1916, aged 20, is framed by portraits of Churchill, Lord Kitchener, Sir John French and Admiral Jellicoe.
ABOVE: Violating the guaranteed neutrality of Belgium was a costly mistake for the Kaiser – and for all Europe. A quarter of a century later, Belgium was again invaded.

Britain was a signatory of the treaty guaranteeing Belgium's neutrality and would fight to defend it. On the evening before Britain declared war, Foreign Secretary Sir Edward Grey famously said, 'The lamps are going out all over Europe, we shall not see them lit again in our life-time.'

Churchill was not the only man fired up at the prospect of war – a patriotic rush of half a million young men all over Britain and the Empire signed up, hoping for the chance to get in on what was expected to be a short, sharp lesson to the nation that had broken the peace. By November, as the news came in of one friend's death after another on the 'Western Front', Winston speculated to his wife about what would happen if all the armies went on strike together and demanded another way to settle things.

The Allies halted the German advance on Paris at the Battle of the Marne in September 1914. This left Germany fighting on two fronts, Eastern and Western – the Kaiser's war plan had failed, but his Army was strong. Both sides dug trenches for 500 miles from the Swiss border to the sea, defending positions from which to launch a counter-attack.

With the British Army 'chewing barbed wire' as each yard of territory back and forth came at the cost of thousands of lives, in February 1915 Churchill bypassed an unconvinced General Kitchener (who was now Minister of War) to fund development of 'landships': a military version of the caterpillar tractor that was a forerunner of the 'tank'. Meanwhile the Royal Naval Air Service was developing not only seaplanes and carrier-borne aircraft but also fighter squadrons of Sopwiths. In October 1914 Churchill ordered an air raid on the German Zeppelin sheds – the first time a plane had ever destroyed a Zeppelin.

Winston had written to his brother Jack in September that he wished he could be with him at the Front: 'I expect I should be very frightened but I would dissemble.' On 3rd October, he was there. The Belgian capital of Brussels had been taken. The port of Antwerp, under siege, was on the point of being abandoned by its government. This could threaten the Channel ports – and therefore Britain; Churchill was ordered to Antwerp to assess the situation.

Delaying the surrender of Antwerp, even for a few days, was vital and Winston cabled back for British Naval troops, offering to resign his post and take charge of the defence of Antwerp personally in absence of a senior British officer. He was told he was needed back in London. Once the British troops arrived, the exhausted Belgians fought on a few more vital days before finally surrendering. Their arrival 'inspired our troops', wrote the King of the Belgians later: 'the delay the Royal Naval Division caused to the enemy was of inestimable service to us.' But at the time, Winston returned to find the Opposition and the newspapers having a field day with what they called Churchill's 'Antwerp blunder', risking the lives of raw recruits on a failed action. It gave, Churchill wrote, 'a handle to my enemies'. Nevertheless, in the week of his 40th birthday, Churchill became a member of Asquith's five-man War Council.

••• ———— •••

Russia's only access to the Mediterranean was via the Bosphorus Strait then the Dardanelles strait. The Ottoman Empire was officially neutral but in September 1914 it closed the Dardanelles, crippling Russia's trade. Churchill embraced the suggestion that an Anglo-French naval force could force the passage.

The Admiralty committed ships, submarines, minesweepers and Marines. These were joined by troops from Australia and New Zealand. But the naval campaign of February and March 1915 found the Gallipoli defences more robust than expected. Kitchener decided to knock them out with a major landing in April – but the defences had been strengthened still further and the Battle of Gallipoli (in which Jack Churchill took part) turned into a long drawn-out bloodbath.

First Sea Lord Prince Louis Battenberg had been driven out of office by anti-German prejudice, even though he had served in the Royal Navy since a boy.

OPPOSITE: A German imagining of the panic caused in London by airships, which operated over the capital from 1915. Defence against them led to the formation of the RAF in 1918.

(He would change his name to Mountbatten, just as the royal family adopted the name Windsor.) Churchill brought back the volatile but brilliant Jacky Fisher as First Sea Lord in Battenberg's place but, under the pressure of the Dardanelles failure, tempers frayed and huge rows erupted between them. Fisher resigned and Churchill departed too, almost immediately: Asquith now needed to form a coalition National Government to run the war and Churchill's replacement at the Admiralty by Conservative Arthur Balfour was part of the price. Sidelined into the sinecure position of Chancellor of the Duchy of Lancaster, Churchill continued to argue in Cabinet against any further action in the Dardanelles until there were sufficient troops to launch a successful assault. But he was powerless.

As instigator of the initial attack Churchill was widely blamed for the rising death toll; political opponents would taunt him with cries of 'Dardanelles!' for decades to come. These would not, significantly, include Labour's Clement Attlee – one of the last officers evacuated from Suvla Bay – who wrote that only 'incredible blunders marred Churchill's fine strategic conception.' But as public anger rose, Churchill was roundly condemned. Clementine said of her husband, 'I thought he would never get over the Dardanelles; I thought he would die of grief.'

Winston found relief from despair in a most unexpected way. The family had leased a small Surrey farmhouse and it was there, at Hoe Farm, that he discovered painting. His brother Jack's wife Gwendoline, visiting with her easel and brushes, saw that painting had sparked an interest and suggested he make a few forays with the children's tin of watercolours; it was Clementine who then bought oil paints (as more suitable to his nature).

However Winston was just sitting by the pond, intimidated by a blank canvas, when their friend Hazel Martyn, an artist married to fellow artist John Lavery, descended on Hoe Farm in her motor car. She demanded Winston's largest brush and, he wrote in amusement, 'Splash into the turpentine, wallop into the blue and the white … several large, fierce strokes and slashes of blue on the absolutely cowering canvas. Anyone could see that it could not hit back.' The canvas, he wrote, 'grinned in helplessness before me. The spell was broken.'

From that moment he was away, his art instinctive and passionate. Finding joy in painting was no small matter for Winston in the summer of 1915. Politically, 'I am finished,' he said, and in November he resigned from the Cabinet, asking to be posted to fight in France. Before he left, he wrote a four-page letter to Clemmie, to be opened 'in the event of my death.' Along with an account of his financial affairs and insurance policy – which should, he said, be sufficient to pay off his debts and leave her reasonably provided for – he urged her to get hold of all his Admiralty papers if she could: 'There is no hurry but some day I should like the truth to be known.' 'Do not grieve for me too much,' he concluded.

F is a Flapper who hoped to assist,
And told Winston Churchill he ought to enlist.

> I am a spirit confident of my rights. Death is only an incident, & not the most important wh happens to us in this state of being. On the whole, especially since I met you my darling one I have been happy, & you have taught me how noble a woman's heart can be. If there is anywhere else I shall be on the look out for you. Meanwhile look forward, feel free, rejoice in Life, cherish the children, guard my memory. God bless you. Good bye.
> W.

OPPOSITE: Clementine with baby Sarah in 1915 or 1916, painted by John Lavery while they were staying at Hoe Farm near Godalming in Surrey away from Zeppelin raids. The families became good friends.
ABOVE: *Punch*'s 1915 *An Alphabet of the War* shows something of the public humiliation that Churchill suffered after being moved from the Admiralty.

His first weeks in France saw him fortified by Clementine's obedient dispatch of everything from a sheepskin sleeping bag, periscope and waterproof trench wading boots to a bottle of peach brandy. (Send 'large slabs of corned beef: stilton cheeses: cream: hams: sardines', he instructed.) His famous face had been greeted by the commanders on the ground with considerable suspicion – but in France, as Winston wrote to Clemmie, 'Amid these surroundings, aided by wet & cold, & every minor discomfort I have found happiness & content such as I have not known for many months.'

At the beginning of 1916 Churchill was given command of a battalion of Scots Fusiliers, demoralised after losing some three-quarters of their officers. Churchill applied himself to the rebuilding of their spirits with team games, a love of sing-song and a leniency in punishment which, when challenged, he defended by showing that offences had gone down as punishments became less peremptory. His adjutant A.D. Gibb wrote that 'no more popular officer ever commanded troops.'

Churchill advised the officers under his command to 'Laugh a little & teach your men to laugh – great good hum'r under fire – war is a game that is played with a smile. If you can't smile, grin. If you can't grin, keep out of the way till you can.'

Troops were rotated in and out of the battle line so he only led his troops in actual trenches for five weeks over five months and these were comparatively quiet ones. But his time at the Front quickly showed the deficiencies in the technical support, such as telephones, given to the fighting men. This war would be 'one of mechanics & brains,' he wrote, the 'mere sacrifice of brave and devoted infantry is no substitute, & never will be.' He felt he could do more good for the troops by putting things right in Westminster but he kept a cheerful face for the men, pouring out his political woes – 'forgive me' – to Clemmie: 'Don't let them … think that I have resigned the game.'

On New Year's Day 1916 he wrote: 'I am vy glad you had Ll.G. to lunch. Do this again: & keep in touch. It really is most important.' And again: 'I have no one but you to act for me. I shd like you to make the seeing of my friends a regular business – like your canteens wh are going so well.' (Clementine was on the YMCA committee to feed munitions workers, setting up and running nine canteens feeding up to 500 workers each.)

The stream of advice and debate between them continued. She was, he told her, 'a very sapient cat to write as you do' and sent 'tenderest love to you & the kittens'. Later that month he confessed: 'I ought to have followed yr counsels in my days of prosperity. Only sometimes they are too negative. I shd have made nothing if I had not made mistakes.'

In March, Winston returned to London on leave. He hadn't planned to attend the Commons but there was an Admiralty debate. He was listened to with care when he made practical suggestions, but when he called (against Clemmie's strongest advice) for the reinstatement of Jacky Fisher he was met with derision. 'These grave public anxieties are very wearing,' she wrote on his return to France, 'When next I see you I hope there will be a little time for us both alone. We are still young, but Time flies, stealing love away.'

Clemmie feared for Winston at the Front, but also feared that a permanent return to civilian life in wartime might be misunderstood. That summer, his battalion was amalgamated with another: only one officer of his rank was required and, after putting considerable energy into finding good postings for his junior officers, Winston was home for good.

From the back benches, he pressed for better management of the war on various fronts. With huge loss of life at sea at the Battle of Jutland (in which the future George VI saw action) and even more on land over bloody months at the Somme, he urged breaking free of both by creating an Air Ministry: 'the air is free and open. There are no entrenchments there.' He fretted that his time away fighting had merely removed him from the chance to have an influence. With his speeches little noted in the press, he took to paid journalism to get his points across. Frustrated, he wrote to his brother at the Front that he writhed hourly, 'not to be able to get my teeth effectively into the Boche' but at the same time he might do '10,000 times as much' in London, if given a chance. 'Jack my dear I am learning to hate.'

At the end of the year Lloyd George wrested control of the National Government from Asquith. A report into the Dardanelles debacle was released which made it clear Churchill was not the villain he had been painted, and in July 1917 the new Prime Minister felt able to defy the press and offer Churchill the

ABOVE: Tear gas was used by both sides on the Western Front, to little effect. Germany then introduced lethal chlorine gas and poison gas use escalated as the war dragged on.

post of Minister of Munitions. (Though the *Morning Post* still poured scorn on this 'unsinkable politician … whose overwhelming conceit led him to imagine he was a Nelson at sea and a Napoleon on land.') This meant another by-election in Dundee, but Clementine successfully campaigned on his behalf.

Soon back at work, Churchill's ministry promoted the further development of the tank, and the importance of air warfare, while he himself flew regularly and hazardously across the Channel to view the fight on the ground. A new way to maim and kill in this war was with poison gas, used first by the Germans, then the French and British. Now at Munitions, his ghastly duty to kill ever more effectively, Churchill thought the idea that gas was uniquely cruel was 'squeamishness' in those who never had to witness the alternative – 'that mechanical scattering of death which the polite nations of the earth have brought to such monstrous perfection' – as he had at Omdurman. Then, he had watched as Dervishes, 'valiant men were struggling on through a hell of whistling metal, exploding shells, and spurting dust', while bullets were 'shearing through flesh, smashing and splintering bone; blood spouted from terrible wounds.' Incapacitating gas delivered in shells from the air to bring a battle to a swift conclusion might even be more merciful.

This was proving a momentous year of the war on all fronts. In April 1917 the Allies were boosted by neutral America's entry into the war after a secret cable from the German Foreign Office to its ambassador in Mexico was deciphered. It promised Mexico an alliance if the unrestricted submarine warfare campaign Germany was about to launch brought the USA into the war. 'Make war together, make peace together, generous financial support' – plus a commitment to help Mexico 'reconquer the lost territory in Texas, New Mexico and Arizona.'

As the first of two million Americans arrived to fight on the Western Front, on the Eastern Front, autumn's Bolshevik Revolution pulled Russian troops out of the war. But it also gave heart to revolutionaries and nationalists across Europe.

The Austro-Hungarian Empire collapsed in October 1918 as its constituent nations sought independence. The following month, with the German Army in retreat, the Navy at Kiel mutinied rather than go to sea in what they suspected was a suicide mission. With the people out on the streets in Berlin, on 9th November the Kaiser abdicated; on the 11th it was all over. Some six or seven million British soldiers had fought in the Great War; a million and a half of them had been wounded, while the bodies of a further 750,000 now enriched the soil 'in some corner of a foreign field'. Now, at the 11th hour of the 11th day of the 11th month, the guns fell silent.

Amidst all this death, Churchill experienced an ironic injection of celebration. On 1st June 1918, Jennie, who had divorced George Cornwallis-West for adultery, had married colonial officer Montagu Porch, three years Winston's junior. Three days after the Armistice, Clementine ceased her canteen work long enough to give birth to their fourth child. Another redhead, they called her Marigold, though she soon became 'Duckadilly'.

A month before, Clementine had written to her husband, urging him to think about their munitions workers (who he employed and she fed) when the fighting stopped. She held up the image of them building garden cities to replace slums in 'Bethnal Green, Newcastle, Glasgow, Leeds etc', with the women workers making the furniture. 'I would like you to be praised as a reconstructive genius as well as for a Mustard Gas Fiend, a Tank juggernaut & a flying Terror.'

Sadly for Clementine, her husband was not about to be moved from Minister of Swords to Minister of Ploughshares. In January 1919 Lloyd George offered Churchill the post of Secretary of State for War and Air.

ABOVE: Female factory workers meet the Minister of Munitions during a visit to Georgetown's shell-filling works near Glasgow on 9th October 1918.

RARA AVIS IN TERRIS.

"Never since the days of Icarus had there been an aviator quite like the right hon. gentleman [Mr. WINSTON CHURCHILL]. He had displayed much sympathy with the Air Force and had almost been one of its martyrs."—*Lord HUGH CECIL.*

PART THREE

—————

1919–39

CHAPTER 7

'The times are very dangerous'

It was a strange time to be Minister of War: 'We are half way between peace and war,' Churchill told the Commons on 3rd March 1919. When he came to write his multi-volume history *The World Crisis*, this volume would be subtitled 'The Aftermath' and dedicated in March 1929 'To All Who Hope'. The fact that 1919–39 is now universally recognised as 'the inter-war years' would have been shattering to all those – Winston included – who believed that this was their opportunity to build a new world that would function without war, once they had cleared up the mess from the last one.

The responsibility for 'enabling the world to get to work again' rested on the victorious Allies, who were themselves exhausted, he told MPs in the debate on Army Estimates. The collapse into chaos of the German, Austrian and Ottoman Empires meant Britain did not yet know how many men it might need on the Rhine or in the Middle East, or for how long. One of the two maxims Churchill derived from 'all history' was: 'Do not disband your army until you have got your terms.'

The other, he said, was: 'Do not be carried away by success into demanding or taking more than is right or prudent.' The Allies were still negotiating in Versailles

OPPOSITE: Even before the Great War, but certainly after, Churchill was alive to the way that air battles would come to determine the future of warfare.

over the territory to be surrendered, conditions to be met and reparations to be paid by Germany. Settle now, said Churchill or 'run a grave risk of having nobody with whom to settle, and of having another great area of the world sink into Bolshevik anarchy.'

At one point in this long debate he apologised for leaving the Chamber, explaining the Under-Secretary helping him at the War Office since the Financial Secretary contracted 'the prevailing epidemic' now had it too. The 'Spanish flu' of 1918–20 would kill 50 million people, surpassing the Great War's 18 million deaths. Though the two were intertwined. The major transit and hospital camp at Étaples in France was probably its bridgehead into Britain – and this month it would reach the village and old Surrey farmhouse where Winston had moved Clemmie and the children for safety during the Zeppelin raids on London.

The children's beloved Scottish nanny Isabelle was gripped by a sudden fever and, in her delirium, took Marigold out of her cot into her own bed. Clementine rescued her baby and took her down to her own bedroom. Unable to get a doctor, she spent the night going up and down between her screaming baby and Isabelle, who 'talked fast & loud in an unearthly voice like a chant for several hours'. At half past five that morning, Isabelle died. Clemmie took the train up to London and wrote to Winston, who was working in France, 'I'm afraid I am in for influenza. My temperature this morning is 102, but perhaps its the sleepless night.' Her own infection was not too severe and, despite her mother's great anxiety, Marigold escaped all harm. Winston, on his return to England, was commanded to stay with Sunny at Blenheim until the danger was past.

The reason Churchill had been pushing for speedy peace terms was so that Britain could end its wartime blockade of German ports. Germany was 'very near starvation', he warned MPs, and threatened 'a collapse of the entire structure of German social and national life.' Germany normally grew 80 per cent of its own food and imported most of the rest over land, but heavy conscription of farm workers, bad harvests and the collapse of government left it in crisis in 1919, needing food aid, not blockade. Churchill said it was 'repugnant to the British nation' to use this weapon of starvation, which fell mainly on 'women and children, upon the old, the weak, and the poor' one moment longer than necessary. And where was the point, he asked, of 'starving everybody into Bolshevism?'

Lloyd George thought Winston had 'Bolshevism on the brain' – that 'his ducal blood revolted against the wholesale elimination of Grand Dukes'. But it was for an infant democracy, not dukes, Churchill mourned. He called the Kerensky

Government that had deposed the Tsar in spring 1917: 'New men, men of very advanced views. With no experience, but men who held views as democratic as those which existed in any of the modern states of Europe.'

Then Germany had transported Lenin back to Russia ('in a sealed truck like a plague bacillus', Churchill wrote later); the Bolsheviks had overthrown the first revolution and had pulled Russia out of the War. Churchill thought diplomacy might bring it back as an ally: 'Lenin and Trotsky are fighting with ropes around their necks,' he wrote; if they were offered aid, and security against the vengeance of counter-revolution, 'they would be non-human not to embrace it'. However, an ineffectual Allied force was already embroiled in the complexities of Russian civil war, peasant uprisings and the nationalist struggles of its old Empire. Churchill

ABOVE: 'You have nothing to lose but your chains.' This Soviet poster from 1919, appealing to the workers of the world, made clear the threat posed to the British Empire.

argued the Allies should either get out of Russia entirely or go in hard, using the latest technology. Including gas bombs, 'pending the general review of the laws of war which no doubt will follow the Peace Conference.'

Amid the mourning for the fallen of the Great War, hopes were high that the modern world could prevent such a stupid thing ever happening again. The League of Nations would be a new, international authority based in Geneva, to arbitrate between member nations in disputes, end slavery, tackle disease etc. Having no armed force of its own, it would mandate members, initially from the victorious Allies, to police its decisions. Any action would require unanimity; no country would have a veto.

Nipping aggression in the bud with collective action would provide 'collective security'. The underlying principles of the League were drawn up by America's President Woodrow Wilson – but the USA itself would not join the League. There was dismay when President Wilson's personal commitment was not ratified by Congress: the majority of American politicians were not prepared to let America be called upon to police foreign trouble-spots, as other powerful victorious Allies like France, Britain, Italy and Japan could be mandated to do.

Churchill was at Versailles, where the peace negotiations were still taking place, in May 1919 – 'on good form' and 'mulish' according to the Chief of the Imperial General Staff. Generally, Winston felt optimistic. The new Royal Air Force should greatly reduce the need for ground troops – and costs – in any future police actions around the Empire or on mandate duty. As Secretary of State for Air, he also put a worrying number of hours into, once again, trying to get his own pilot's licence, surviving two crash landings in the summer of 1919 alone. In August, he persuaded the Cabinet to adopt a 'Ten Year Rule': the defence budget to be set on the assumption Britain would not be involved in a major war in the next ten years.

The Cabinet that Winston was part of was not a Liberal one. Though Lloyd George was Prime Minister, the 1918 election had given him only a third of the MPs of his Conservative and Unionist coalition partner, which made following or promoting the Liberal pro-Irish Home Rule policy impossible. Meanwhile three-quarters of Irish constituencies had voted for Éamon de Valera's Sinn Féin, whose MPs refused to take up their seats in Westminster and assembled in Dublin as the 'Dáil Éireann' – Irish Parliament. Both Parliament and party were outlawed and an escalating guerilla war began.

The eruption of what the English called 'The Irish Question' into Churchill's life had a savage irony. His earliest childhood memories were of Ireland: his grandfather the Lord–Lieutenant; Mr Burke, who had given him a drum then been stabbed to death in Phoenix Park; Mrs Everest's mortal fear of Fenians. Writing later with a historian's eye, Churchill called it 'The Curse of Cromwell', whose brutality in Ireland had 'cut new gulfs between the nations and the creeds,' he wrote, and healing them, 'baffled the skill and loyalties of successive generations.' It had baffled his father and grandfather; now it would baffle him, with the War Office's attempt to help deal with what he saw as troublemakers for civil society only ratcheting up the conflict.

With policemen being intimidated and killed, Churchill organised a more militarised force to back them up. The Royal Irish Constabulary Special Reserves, whose uniforms earned them the nickname 'Black and Tans', were recruited in England from recently demobilised ex-servicemen. The official Irish administration at Dublin Castle recruited ex-officers similarly for the separate Royal Irish Constabulary Auxiliaries. Both forces straddled the dividing line between civilian policing and armed troops, with inevitable results. The single worst day of bloodshed was on 21st November 1920, 'Bloody Sunday', which began with the assassination of 14 British intelligence agents by the Irish Republican Army, followed by the beating to death of three Republican prisoners, and a group of Reserves and Auxiliaries firing randomly into the crowd at a Gaelic football match, killing 12 instantly and wounding 65.

'Black and Tans' was now a name as hated as Cromwell in Ireland, and the Churchill name with it. The constant presence at his side for many years to come of Special Branch detective constable Walter Thompson was a reminder that Churchill's name had been found on a kidnap list and for months he slept with a revolver beside him.

As so often, his wife's intervention was forthright in her disapproval of Winston's actions, when she felt it was warranted. 'She had very strong views and he didn't always agree with them,' said their daughter Mary. 'And I don't think she was necessarily always right. The point is, she had the capacity and the will to tussle with him about politics and public affairs.' On 18 February 1921, she did not sugar the pill when talking about his new job: 'Do my darling use your influence *now* for some sort of moderation or at any rate justice in Ireland – Put yourself in the place of the Irish … It always makes me unhappy & disappointed when I see you *inclined* to take for granted that the rough iron-fisted 'hunnish' way will prevail …'

Churchill was now, and had been since New Year's Day, Colonial Secretary. He had taken Clementine, who was extremely run down, on a short holiday in

the South of France and she stayed there on his return, the letters flying between them full of politics, money worries and family news. 'The so-called Duckadilly marched into my room this morning,' Winston wrote, 'apparently in blooming health. It was a formal visit & she had no special communication to make. But the feeling was good.' Randolph was at school and, though the other two girls should have been too, they were recuperating in Broadstairs from a winter of coughs and colds. Winston wrote his letter on a visit to Chequers, recently donated to be the Prime Minister's country residence: 'Here I am,' he wrote. 'You wd like to see this place – Perhaps you will some day!'

Neither of the main projects in Churchill's in tray during his 20 months at the Colonial Office were strictly colonial at all. One was Ireland, where he would be part of the team negotiating a peace treaty with Sinn Féin. The other was the Middle East, where Britain was to be given 25-year mandates by the League of Nations to administer and police some former Ottoman colonies for the benefit of their native peoples as a 'sacred trust of civilization'. While these work responsibilities naturally weighed heavily in 1921, the year would see, in addition, heavy personal burdens fall on Winston.

In March, Clementine went with him to Cairo and Jerusalem for a Middle East Conference. This was Churchill's first attempt to try to resolve the intractable issues that arose from conflicting promises made by the British Government during the war about what would happen to the region if the Ottoman Empire fell. Before the discovery of oil in 1908, Western interest in these lands had been minimal; now British and French Mandates complicated the conflicts of the region.

Within weeks of their return in April, the Churchills faced the first of three family tragedies that year. Clementine's brother Bill, beloved by them both, committed suicide in Paris at the age of thirty-three, and Clementine rushed to France to support her mother.

In May, Winston's own mother, still at sixty-seven a striking and fashionable woman, tripped in her high-heeled shoes and a compound ankle fracture led first to blood poisoning, then gangrene. Jennie took the news that the leg must be amputated stoically. But she had barely been declared out of danger after the operation when she suffered a major haemorrhage and, on 29th June, died. A remarkable relationship had come to an end. 'We worked together on even terms,'

OPPOSITE: Churchill in formal attire as Secretary of State for the Colonies, accompanied by his wife. Though his time in the role was short, it was full of personal and political drama.

Winston wrote, 'More like brother and sister than mother and son. At least so it seems to me. And so it continued to the end.'

But Winston worked on. If Middle East conflict was Britain's newest responsibility, Ireland was one of its oldest. On 11th July 1921 a truce was signed, and Michael Collins, director of intelligence for the Irish Republican Army as well as Finance Minister, came to London at the head of the Sinn Féin delegation. Collins knew that 'Once a truce is agreed and we come out into the open, it is extermination for us if the truce should fail.' He was, as Churchill might have said, negotiating with a noose around his neck.

Michael Collins and Churchill developed an unlikely relationship during the negotiations: combative but infused with respect. When Collins came to dinner and angrily claimed the British had put a £5,000 bounty on his head, Churchill showed him the framed Boer poster that had priced his own at £25.

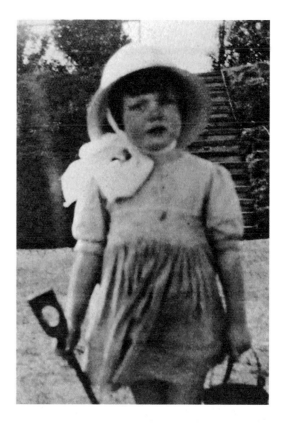

In August, Winston and Clemmie were summoned by cable to Broadstairs. Marigold – 'the Duckadilly' – who was holidaying at the seaside with her nanny, had developed yet another sore throat. It had turned to septicaemia; she was very ill. They were at her bedside on 23rd August when, not yet three, Marigold died. Clementine screamed, said Winston, 'Like an animal in pain.' A month later, in Dundee to give a speech, Winston found himself alone in a cheerful fishing and shooting party. 'I keep on feeling the hurt of the Duckadilly,' he wrote to his wife, and she wrote back that she had taken the children to the grave, where a little white butterfly had settled on the flowers growing there. A year later, Winston wrote that it was still 'a gaping wound, whenever one touches it & removes the bandages & plasters of daily life.'

The Irish peace treaty signed on 6th December 1921 led to the partitioning of Ireland: the six counties of the North were given the option of opting out of the Irish Free State, which was to be recognised as a self-governing dominion within the British Empire. Collins judged it: 'not the ultimate freedom … but the freedom to achieve it,' but knew not everyone would agree. 'The unity of Ireland … is surely the goal to which we must all look steadfastly,' Churchill wrote to him, 'Plain folk must have time to take things in and adjust their minds to what has happened.' He added a postscript: 'I hope you are taking good care of yourself and your colleagues. The times are very dangerous.' Collins wrote that, in signing the treaty, he had signed his own death warrant. He was right: the Free State erupted into civil war, and Collins was dead within the year.

'I hope you are taking good care of yourself and your colleagues. The times are very dangerous.'

OPPOSITE: Seen here with Clementine in the summer of 1919, Winston's mother, like his daughter, fell victim to septicaemia.
ABOVE: Marigold, known to her parents as 'the Duckadilly', died during her third summer and her loss remained 'a gaping wound' for Winston.

CHAPTER 8

'The garden of England'

For the Churchills, 1922 was a year of new beginnings. Winston had first seen Chartwell Manor, a house in 80 acres of land, not long after the death of his mother. He fell in love with the spectacular views towards the Weald: 'The garden of England … strawberries, cherries, raspberries and plums. Lovely! I always wanted to live in Kent.' A legacy from a distant cousin prompted him to enquire again a year later and, yes, it was still available.

Clementine's reaction was more cautious. Yes, she loved 'the house on the hill' but the work required was terrifying; upkeep costs might be heavy; could it ever have enough bedrooms to invite Jack's family …? However it offered Winston, the child of Blenheim, a sense of place, space and strong roots deeply anchored into the English landscape. Winston was in love.

The couple conceived again within months of Marigold's death and on 15th September 1922, their fifth and final child, Mary, was born. In the last week of Clementine's pregnancy, Winston put in an offer for the house without telling her – a deception for which she never altogether forgave him. The children felt differently. With their mother still in bed after the delivery, Winston drove Randolph, Diana and Sarah down to picnic in the romantically overgrown grounds, and waited until they begged him to buy the place before confessing he had already done so.

OPPOSITE: The appeal of 'the house on the hill' was less evident when Churchill first bought it.
RIGHT: Chartwell still displays the portrait of Sarah and Diana that was painted there by Charles Sims.

He got the house for £5,000, but Clementine was right: Chartwell would be a constant drain on their finances. The Tudor farmhouse at its core, where Henry VIII is said to have stayed while courting Anne Boleyn at nearby Hever Castle, was overlaid by a carapace of Victorian excrescences prey to damp and to dry rot (the architect Churchill hired called the place 'weary of its own ugliness'). But Chartwell would be, for the rest of Winston's days, a beloved family home and pet project – yet another life's work for a man who always seemed able to fit in one more.

Within weeks of the purchase, Lloyd George's administration fell and, wrote Churchill, 'In the twinkling of an eye I found myself without an office, without a seat, without a party and without an appendix.' The appendectomy, still then a dangerous operation, meant Clementine had to travel with baby Mary to Dundee, campaigning until Winston was strong enough be carried to meetings in an invalid chair. One campaigner described her demeanour as that of an aristocrat going to the guillotine in a tumbril; when she appeared wearing a string of pearls, some women spat at her. Winston lost his seat as part of a wider Liberal disaster. Labour now had more MPs than Asquith and Lloyd George put together, and the Conservatives had double that. Churchill's chances of ever again becoming a Liberal MP had dwindled to virtually nothing.

But he was still a writer, and 1923 saw publication of the first volume of his account of the Great War. (It was said that 'Winston has written a book about himself and called it *The World Crisis*.') In 1923, he stood as a Liberal and lost again, this time in Leicester West. In the March 1924 by-election for Westminster Abbey, he stood on a 'Constitutionalist' ticket, billing himself as 'Independent Anti-Socialist'. His flamboyant electioneering style – he drove round London in a coach and four with a trumpeter on the box – went down much better than it had in Dundee, but he lost to the Conservative by an agonising 43 votes.

He was still writing, of course, and his 1924 essay called 'Shall We All Commit Suicide?' showed he still had an eye on international politics – and a pretty sophisticated understanding of what any Second Great War could look like. 'Without having improved appreciably in virtue or enjoying wiser guidance,' he warned, mankind now had the tools in its hands to 'accomplish its own extermination.'

OPPOSITE: Winston painted his 1927 self-portrait with Chartwell guests (above) from a photograph taken in what was known, both then and now (below) as 'the breakfast room'. In truth, he and Clemmie breakfasted in their bedrooms. He held strong views on dining chairs – a house needed at least 20: upright so a few could draw together sociably, but with arms to prevent crowding and elbowing.

In 1921 the Duke of Westminster had introduced Churchill to Frederick Lindemann, an Oxford physics professor with a knack of explaining advanced science in layman's terms. So when Churchill asks his reader whether 'a bomb no bigger than an orange' might be found to 'possess secret power to … blast a township at a stroke,' he wasn't just being fanciful.

A year before the League of Nations' worldwide ban on chemical and biological weapons, Churchill no longer saw gas as a lesser evil to anything, writing that, in terms of chemical weapons: 'only the first chapter has been written of a terrible book'.

As war became global annihilation, world peace was the only rational solution. Looking back, Churchill would identify 1925 as the high point of progress towards it, when the Locarno Treaties began normalising relations with the democratic Weimar Republic in Germany, in return for its promise never to go to war. But from then on, he would later judge, the world marched backwards.

In the autumn of 1924, he stood again as a Constitutionalist, this time on the fringes of London in Epping. Stanley Baldwin ensured no Conservative stood against him and Churchill romped home with a majority of almost 10,000. The new Prime Minister invited him for a meeting. Clementine, the staunch Liberal, was assured that if the Tories wanted to lure her husband back, it would take a great offer to tempt him. It was one not even he dreamt of. Chancellor of the Exchequer – the pinnacle of his father's career. He still had his father's robes.

Churchill may or may not have actually uttered the words 'Anyone can rat, but it takes a certain amount of ingenuity to re-rat.' But it sums up the ebullient defiance with which he crossed the floor of the House again.

With wide ministerial experience, he merrily poached on the preserve of other departments. The First Sea Lord wrote to his wife: 'That extraordinary fellow Winston has gone mad' when he rejected demands for more warships in this new peaceful world, since they would leave nothing for the taxpayer or 'for social reform'. Health Minister Neville Chamberlain said, 'What a brilliant creature he is … But not for all the joys of Paradise would I be a member of his staff! Mercurial!'

Churchill moved into 11 Downing Street with his old Liberal principles intact. His first budget saw improved pensions – what he described as 'ambulances of state aid' for 'stragglers' and raised Death Duties. But that 1925 budget is famous for just one thing – a disastrous budgetary mistake that he later confessed was his 'biggest blunder.' Ironically, while returning the British Pound to the Gold Standard sounds stereotypically 'Churchillian' it was done against his better judgement. The Governor of the Bank of England, Treasury, and Finance Select

Committee all said this would make the pound strong; he thought it would make British industry uncompetitive – but after a secret two-month battle allowed himself to be persuaded.

The move caused a recession, with the coal industry particularly badly hit. Mine owners responded by cutting wages. At the urging of the trade unions, Churchill backed a nine-month wage subsidy while a Royal Commission looked into the future of the industry. But its report in March 1926 recommended reforms – and a wage reduction of 13½ per cent.

The Trades Union Congress backed the miners' current wage with a General Strike. Millions of key workers withdrew their labour. As the Army helped to break picket lines at the London docks, what Churchill would call his 'natural pugnacity' was released: he wanted food lorries escorted by tanks and overseen by machine guns. It was, he growled, much harder to feed a nation than to wreck it. 'He thinks he is Napoleon,' J.C.C. Davidson wrote to Baldwin. 'But curiously enough, the men who have been printing all their life in the various processes happen to know more about their job than he does.' Davidson was managing the newspaper that Winston founded and edited while the rest of the press were generally unable to print. Within the strike's nine-day duration, the *British Gazette* reached a circulation of over two million and Churchill managed to infuriate other proprietors by commandeering their newsprint; his own printers by telling them how to run the presses; and the editorial staff by 'changing commas and full stops'. His attempts to get control of the fledgling BBC too were seen off by the equally formidable Scot John Reith, who Churchill would refer to as 'That Wuthering Height' (Reith was around a foot taller than Churchill at six foot six).

'He thinks he is Napoleon, but curiously enough, the men who have been printing all their life in the various processes happen to know more about their job than he does.'

The *British Gazette* carried the Prime Minister's message that: 'The general strike is a challenge to the parliament and is the road to anarchy.' That had never been the TUC's aim – it was trying to ensure miners could feed their families. Even George V said, 'Try living on their wages before you judge them.' But in the end the TUC backed down. The miners' strike continued for a further six months, and when the men returned – those who were allowed to return – it was to longer hours for less money.

Churchill finished volume three of *The World Crisis* and marked this temporary pause for breath with a family holiday. In Sicily he viewed an eruption of Vesuvius;

in Rome he twice met Mussolini. Public men meeting on a friendly basis was one of the ways international suspicion could be diminished, he said in a press release. He had been impressed by the facts and figures on the Italian wage-earners' position and said, if he were Italian he would have been with Mussolini from the start, 'But in England … we have our way of doing things.'

He was writing again through the summer of 1928. He told Baldwin that he had spent 'a delightful month – building a cottage & dictating a book: 200 bricks and 2,000 words per day.' His pleasure in bricklaying, both its meditative quality and sense of achievement, was genuine. While Harrow was a very good school, he wrote in the book he was dictating as he laid his bricks:

> I would far rather have been apprenticed as a bricklayer's mate, or run errands
> as a messenger boy, or helped my father to dress the front windows of a grocer's
> shop. It would have been real; it would have been natural; it would have taught me

ABOVE: Mussolini's Fascism was the talk of the 1920s, and its authoritarian swagger became, in the 1930s, a model for Oswald Mosley, founder of the British Union of Fascists. Churchill himself (above right, talking to footballers) remained steadfastly committed all his life to wooing 'the little man … making a little cross on a little bit of paper' who was at the heart of British democracy.

OPPOSITE: At Chartwell, Winston took up bricklaying and worked on many outbuildings, including a small cottage for daughter Mary, who here is working alongside him.

more; and I should have done it much better. Also I should have got to know my father, which would have been a joy to me.

In the House of Commons, a Government Bill was passed in 1928 giving women the vote on the same terms as men. The papers all dubbed the following year's poll the 'Flapper Election'.

The results were catastrophic for Winston. While he kept his own seat, the Conservatives were out of power – Britain had a Labour Government. Could the Chancellorship have been for Winston, as for his father, the peak of his career? Would he now end his days, like Lord Randolph, in the wilderness?

CHAPTER 9

'Take things as they come'

Churchill's autobiographical volume *My Early Life* received a warm reception in 1930 for its wit and charm, though its tale of Winston's youth and Imperial adventures as 'a child of the Victorian era' now seemed to mock his youthful promise. Out of office, he now took on the writing of a biography of his ancestor the 1st Duke of Marlborough. But as he approached his 56th birthday, all things conspired to impress upon him that History had no further need of Winston Churchill except as a recorder of past glories.

Still, there was a future to think about. Winston accepted a transatlantic lecture tour, his first since 1900. He was an exceptionally well-paid writer, commanding £200, even £500 for one article (when a bricklayer earned 15 shillings a day). But juggling advances from publishers with taxes collected in arrears meant he was always living on borrowed time – and Chartwell was an expensive mistress. America would be a rich source and market for his journalism.

He took along his brother Jack, son Randolph and Jack's son John, courtesy of Canadian Pacific, which provided both Atlantic crossing and a luxurious private railway carriage – with shorthand secretary – in return for a series of lectures *en route*. Churchill met the Canadian Prime Minister and, excited by the possibilities on this side of the Atlantic, wired his publisher to send his next royalty cheque – in advance – directly to his stockbroker. He wrote to Clemmie he had made £6,000 so far and spent almost nothing. In California he was entertained at San Simeon by newspaper magnate William Randolph Hearst and bought more stock. In every big hotel, he told Clemmie: 'You go and sit and watch the figures being marked up on slates every few minutes.'

On the set of *City Lights*, Charlie Chaplin gave up a day's shooting to entertain them and they discussed Winston writing him a script about the young

OPPOSITE: Churchill's trip to America yielded the ultimate fisherman's tale of beginner's luck. Fishing off Catalina Island with local banker Ben R. Meyer, he landed a monster marlin swordfish.

Napoleon. 'You cd not help liking him,' he told Clemmie. 'The boys were fascinated by him. He is a marvellous comedian – bolshy in politics – delightful in conversation.'

The party toured Civil War battlefields before Washington DC, where Winston saw President Hoover, then New York, arriving on 24th October – Black Thursday. That morning the New York Stock Exchange lost 11 per cent on the opening bell but rallied by the end of the day; Churchill's broker still advised him to buy. Friday's trading was even worse and at his farewell dinner, Winston was toasted with: 'Friends and *former* millionaires.' But it was only at sea that the ship's ticker-tape revealed the full extent of his losses. In the Wall Street Crash that bankrupted millions and ushered in the Great Depression, Winston had lost half of everything he had – including his advance for *Marlborough*, for which he had written not one word.

He dreaded telling Clemmie, but blurted it out the moment she met him at Waterloo Station. They closed off most of the rooms at Chartwell, living in a staff cottage in the grounds that daughter Mary remembered as agreeably cosy.

His prodigious energy quickly restored the family to the way of life they had hitherto enjoyed. Mary recalled the magic of Christmas at Chartwell in the thirties, tobogganing down slopes and ice-skating on the lake. Frequent visitor Johnny recalled his uncle playing charades (at times of his own choosing). Winston warned luncheon guests, 'You'll find us all bunged up with brats.'

ABOVE: Chartwell would welcome Chaplin (above, far right) in 1931, repaying his Hollywood hospitality (below). While in England, 'bolshy' Chaplin also met Gandhi and his family in London's East End.

On 29th January 1931, *The New York Times* reported, 'A new and interesting paragraph in the history of British political personalities was written tonight when Winston Churchill sent a letter to Stanley Baldwin proffering his resignation as a member of the Conservative leader's "shadow cabinet".' Later that year, when the Labour Party split over how to rescue the crashed economy, Baldwin joined Ramsay MacDonald's National Coalition. But there would be no place for Winston Churchill. His views on self-government for India would place him outside mainstream politics and convince many that Churchill was now an old man completely behind the times.

The British Empire was his 'alpha and omega', he would tell the Soviet Ambassador Ivan Maisky, more than once, during this decade. But it was no longer the one into which he had been born, setting its bounds 'wider still and wider'. The story had changed for the 'Mother Country': her children were growing up into self-governing dominions under the Crown. The Irish Free State was recognised in 1922. Canada, Australia, New Zealand and South Africa were due to follow at the end of 1931 and India was now up for discussion in London. Baldwin's support for these discussions had been Churchill's resignation issue.

Churchill's opposition to self-government for India has usually been written off – at the time and since – as no more than an old man's racist or romantic illusion about the Raj. But as so often, even when wrong, his thinking had its own internal rationale and looked forward as well as back. The little spinning wheel Mohandas K. Gandhi, now 'the Mahatma', brought with him to the London Conference was not, to Churchill, some strange eccentricity but a clear economic warning for the British mill towns that he had represented for more than 20 years.

The French would not give up their colonies, he argued, nor the Dutch or Italians – as for Japan, it was seeking more. (Japan invaded Manchuria on 18th September 1931 and the League of Nations' failure to do anything to protect it was a major demonstration of the weakness of the League's promise of 'collective security'.) Churchill called those ranged against him – the majority – 20 years behind the times. 'In my view,' he wrote in 1933 to a future Viceroy of India, 'England is now beginning a new period of struggle and fighting for its life, and the crux of it will be not only the retention of India but a much stronger assertion of commercial rights.'

'England is now beginning a new period of struggle and fighting for its life, and the crux of it will be not only the retention of India but a much stronger assertion of commercial rights.'

What the Indian people got on the side of the Imperial bargain, he believed, was good governance. 'There are 50 Indias,' he said, and under what Churchill spoke of as Britain's 'appeasing sceptre', all lived together peacefully – and could, going forward, as devolved state governments. But replace what was essentially an empire in itself with a single, independent state, and he feared that peaceful co-existence could be shattered.

Such paternalism was the proudest claim of the progressive Imperialists of Churchill's youth. A book from the 1880s that he knew well had famously said 'we seem, as it were, to have conquered half the world in a fit of absence of mind' – but it also explained the Imperial idea of morality.

HIS MORNING EXERCISE.
THE LONE EX-MINISTER UPON HIS ELEPHANT.
[Mr. WINSTON CHURCHILL—not without a large body of Conservative support in the country—continues to demonstrate his opposition to the policy of the National Government.]

When India was run by the rapacious and corrupt 'nabobs' of Britain's East India Company, J.R. Seeley wrote in *The Expansion of England*, 'there never was a Government so wholly indifferent to the welfare of its subjects.' However, since Westminster took over the Company's assets and responsibilities in 1858, he wrote: 'The Government is now as sincerely paternal as any Government can be.' This was what Churchill described in a speech at the Royal Albert Hall: 'Our Duty to India'.

But the world had moved on since young Winston's uneventful posting in Bangalore, and there had been a change of heart at the heart of Empire. A million Indians had fought in the Great War, more than 60,000 had sacrificed their lives, and George V's royal proclamation of 1919 approved a new law that entrusted: 'the elected representative of the people with a definite share in the Government and

ABOVE: In the early 1930s, India was regarded as Churchill's political hobby-horse – or hobby-elephant. This helped to paint him as out of touch on other issues too.

points the way to full responsible Government hereafter.' In that same year of 1919 occurred what Churchill, then Minister of War, called, 'an extraordinary event, a monstrous event, an event which stands in singular and sinister isolation'.

The Amritsar massacre of unarmed Indians at the command of a British officer clearly exposed the limits of paternalism. The officer could have probably dispersed the crowd peacefully, he told the enquiry that was held afterwards, 'but they would have come back again and laughed, and I would have made, what I consider, a fool of myself.' Rabindranath Tagore, India's first Nobel laureate, renounced his knighthood in protest at the massacre. And Mohandas K. Gandhi, recently returned to India from South Africa, took up a relentlessly non-violent campaign for independence from Britain that aimed to unite all Indians. This won growing support in Britain and grudging respect in Westminster, hence his invitation to London in 1931.

He came representing the Indian National Congress, which included more conventional politicians like Harrow-educated Jawaharlal Nehru. Care had been taken to include at the Conference representatives of the Indian princes and maharajahs who nominally ruled half of India, the country's many religions and all sectors of society: well over a hundred participants in all. India was definitely on the road to becoming a Dominion now, everyone in the National Government agreed. (Though, privately, Health Minister Neville Chamberlain said it would take another 50 years to achieve.)

The 1935 Government of India Act that emerged from the London Conference would give India a devolved government, though with British veto; a few weeks after it passed, Churchill invited Gandhi's friend Ghanshyam Das Birla to lunch at Chartwell. It was, Birla wrote to Gandhi, 'one of my most pleasant experiences'. Churchill did three-quarters of the talking, with the rest divided between himself and Mrs Churchill but he enjoyed it – 'it was never boring'.

'Mr Gandhi has gone very high in my esteem since he stood up for the untouchables,' Churchill said. He did not like this new law, but now it *was* law, 'make it a success'. His test of success? 'Improvement in the lot of the masses, morally as well as materially. I do not care whether you are more or less loyal to Great Britain. I do not care about education, but give the masses more butter. I stand for butter.'

He had plenty of advice to offer, of course: reduce the number of cows; improve the breed; provide a good bull for every village, 'Make every tiller of the soil his own landlord.' He was sorry he could not meet with Gandhi in 1931, he said, but hoped they would meet again one day. On his return, Birla wrote that Gandhi said he remembered Mr Churchill from the Colonial Office. And that he had somehow always thought he could 'rely on his sympathy and goodwill'.

••• ——— •••

Another American lecture tour was planned for 1931: 40 lectures on 'The Destiny of the English-Speaking People': a new idea Churchill was developing into a book. This time he took Clementine and Diana and they sailed to New York. Where, looking the wrong way while crossing Fifth Avenue on 13th December, he walked straight into the path of an oncoming car.

Amid the chaos and pain, in a 'small chamber or sanctum wherein all is orderly and undisturbed' he calmly considered: 'I have been run over by a motorcar in America. All those worries about being late are now swept away. They do not matter any more. Here is a real catastrophe. Perhaps it is the end.'

Within three days Winston cabled the son of the owner of the *Daily Mail*: 'Have complete recollection of whole event & can produce literary gem about 2,400 words.' His convalescence in Prohibition America was eased by a doctor's prescription for alcoholic spirits, especially at mealtimes, ('minimum requirements would be 250 cubic centimetres'). The lesson he took from his near-death experience was that: 'Nature is merciful … live dangerously; take things as they come; dread naught, all will be well.' On his return to London he was greeted with a luxury Daimler, a gift from more than 100 well-wishers.

His monetary and political losses and now this 'terrible physical injury' brought him low. But he would, before too long, be standing again at his lectern in Chartwell or striding around the room, not always fully clothed, while his team of researchers, first-drafters and stenographers ministered to his needs. Churchill often dictated long into the night, having perfected his pattern of two baths and two working days per day, separated by a short night's sleep and the after-lunch *siesta* that may have been suggested by his time in Cuba.

In 1932, working on Marlborough, Winston took Clementine, Randolph, Sarah and the 'Prof' with him on a research trip to see the Blenheim battlefield in Bavaria. Where, in nearby Munich, Winston Churchill made a date with destiny. Perhaps history had one more job left for him after all.

The party agreed to meet Adolf Hitler for tea in the restaurant of the hotel where they were staying. The Leader came daily around five, they were assured by his Foreign Press Chief Putzi Hanfstaengl, who had joined their table and offered to make the introduction. Hitler had just lost the Presidential election to Great War hero General von Hindenburg. Churchill had little idea of his politics and none of his character, but was happy enough to meet the leader of the National Socialist German Workers' Party.

He had no problem with anyone standing up for Germany, Churchill said to Putzi over dinner, but why 'is your chief so violent about the Jews? … What is the sense of being against a man simply because of his birth? How can any man help how he is born?' He never got to ask the question in person: Hitler found that he could not make the appointed day after all – nor any day during the remainder of their stay. According to Hanfstaengl, Hitler dismissed Churchill as not worth the time: 'What part does Churchill play? He's in opposition and no one pays any attention to him.'

OPPOSITE: 'Winter Sunshine', awarded first prize in an amateur art competition in 1925, shows Churchill's fierce affection for his beloved Chartwell. But leaving it to go abroad had awoken his fears that the 'terrible engine' of war might revive.
ABOVE: Churchill recognised that the German military still sought revenge for their Great War defeat, and now lent their support to Hitler (pictured here in traditional *lederhosen*) in the hope of rearmament.

Life at Chartwell

The Visitors' Book still displayed
in the hall at Chartwell represents
a who's who of public life between
the wars. Leading politicians and
newspaper barons Lords Beaverbrook
and Camrose rubbed shoulders with
celebrities like Charlie Chaplin and
Laurence Olivier. T.E. Lawrence –
'Lawrence of Arabia' – would arrive by
motorcycle, donning the robes of an
Arabian warlord for dinner.

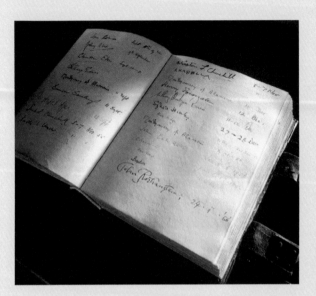

Churchill wrote 'the stomach
governs the world', and the lavish
hospitality of Chartwell was a useful
weapon in his political armoury. While
Clementine filled the house with
scented flowers, Churchill might be
found reliving the charge at Omdurman
for his dinner guests with pepper pots
and salt cellars amid generous supplies
of Pol Roger champagne.

When the guests departed,
Chartwell remained for Winston both a
refuge and a passion. The architect who
had helped remodel it reflected that
'No client I have ever had, considering
his well-filled life, has ever spent more
time, trouble, or interest in the making
of his home than did Mr Churchill.'

Long after the rebuilding of the
house was completed, one project

after another transformed the gardens. Clementine's great pleasure was the tennis court; Winston's the swimming pool – dug and heated to bath temperature by two coke-fired boilers. Lady Diana Cooper remembered bathing in the chill, pouring rain at seven in the evening and how, when no staff could be found to do it, 'darling old schoolboy' Winston almost suffered an apoplexy in his efforts to stoke the range himself.

Winston himself built an enchanting miniature cottage for his daughter Mary, who laid the foundation stone with great ceremony in the summer of 1928. He also wallowed in stinking black mud helping to landscape the lakes. Lorryloads of great rocks created a natural-looking waterfall and rockery and the pools were

OPPOSITE: Chartwell's Visitors' Book (above) records the arrival of the famous. Winston (below) in custom-made 'rompers' (later referred to as 'siren suits') welcomed nuclear physicist Albert Einstein for lunch in 1933, and 'The Prof' arranged for Einstein to lecture in Oxford. This was Einstein's last trip to Europe – he took a university post in America when Germany excluded Jews from public office.
ABOVE: 'I bought Chartwell for that view,' Churchill told a secretary late in life, by which time it included some of his own handiwork: the brickwork of his painting studio.

filled with ornamental fish from Harrods, which Winston loved to paint as he sat in a simple garden chair.

Although the phrase 'art therapy' would not be coined (by someone else) until the 1940s, Winston Churchill had already discovered the therapeutic value of becoming absorbed in the process of painting. 'Painting came to my rescue in a most trying time,' he wrote in one of a series of magazine articles in the 1920s (later published as *Painting as a Pastime*) in which he tried to express 'the gratitude I feel' to art and to pass on his passion to others.

His mother Jennie called painting 'an opiate' for him, but it swiftly moved from being an escape from the sorrow of the Dardanelles to a positive choice, whatever his mood. 'I must say I like bright colours,' he wrote, 'I rejoice with the brilliant ones, and am genuinely sorry for the poor browns.' When he got to heaven, he said, he expected to spend a considerable portion of his first million years in painting; and expected to find an even brighter palette there.

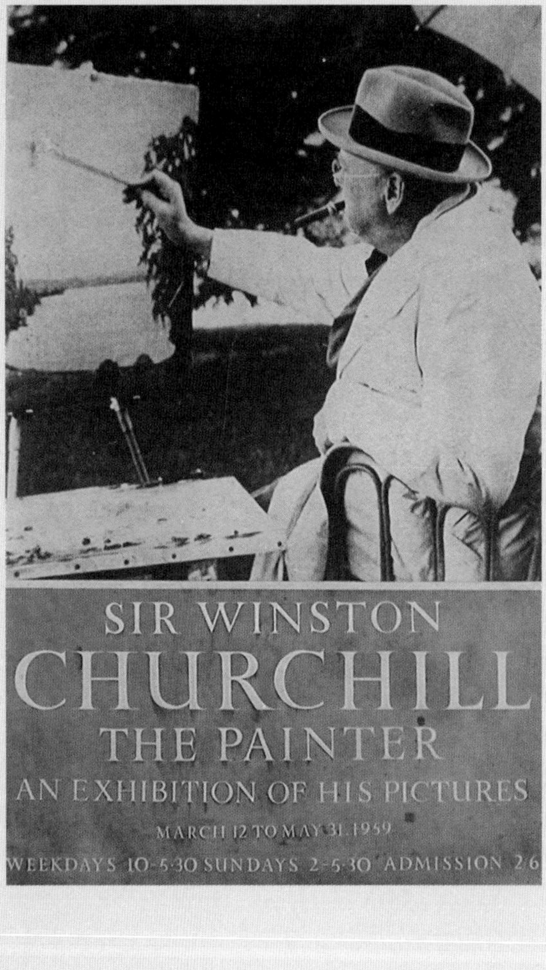

SIR WINSTON
CHURCHILL
THE PAINTER
AN EXHIBITION OF HIS PICTURES
MARCH 12 TO MAY 31 1959
WEEKDAYS 10-5.30 SUNDAYS 2-5.30 ADMISSION 2/6

Though his work was chosen for Royal Academy Summer Exhibitions (initially submitted under the pseudonym 'David Winter'), he never ranked himself among the 'real painters' who joined the visitors to his self-built Chartwell studio, such as William Nicholson and Paul Maze. He remained modest about 'my little daubs'. 'We must not be ambitious,' he wrote. 'We cannot aspire to masterpieces. We may content ourselves with a joy-ride in a paintbox.'

OPPOSITE: For half a century, painting in oils – often outdoors at Chartwell – was a source of deep joy for Churchill.

ABOVE: Winston's paintings, at home or abroad, revel in colour and light. Clockwise from top left: Chartwell's golden orfe fascinated him; Marrakesh ('simply the nicest place on Earth to spend an afternoon'); self-portrait of the artist; the drawing room, where he received 'real artists' among his visitors with an unaccustomed humility about his own 'little daubs'.

CHAPTER 10

'Tell the truth to the British people'

On 10th November, the day before Armistice Day 1932, a fractious Commons debate bemoaned the slow progress of the World Disarmament Conference involving the League of Nations and the USA at Geneva. MPs and ministers squabbled about the true road to lasting peace. Should Britain stand by Versailles and keep Germany disarmed? Or should new treaties give every nation, including Germany, exactly the same amount of weapons? France maintained the strongest army in Europe – was that fair? What even counted as an offensive or a defensive weapon? Might civil aircraft be internationalised, to prevent any one nation developing military air capacity?

Churchill was away ill, so could not respond immediately to the memorable speech with which Stanley Baldwin set the tone for Britain's international policy in the 1930s. Winding up what he called a 'most interesting debate' for the National Government, Baldwin said, 'Few of my colleagues around me here, probably, will see another great war.'

It was for younger men, he warned (Baldwin was 65), to decide if the terrible weapons that had been proposed for the last war were ever used: 'The future is in their hands. But when the next war comes, and European civilisation is wiped out, as it will be and by no force more than by that force, then do not let them lay the blame upon the old men.'

Newspaper headlines the next day splashed Baldwin's warning to the 'man in the street … there is no power on earth that can protect him from being bombed, whatever people may tell him. The bomber will always get through.'

Churchill knew Baldwin's combination of alarmism and complacency was wrong, perhaps catastrophically wrong. Thirteen days later, Churchill spoke in the

OPPOSITE: Churchill is stretchered to a nursing home. A recurrence of salmonella poisoning contracted in Europe kept him away from the vital 1932 Commons debate on disarmament.

House of Commons for over an hour. In a speech of more than 7,000 words, he presented the world of 1932 with two futures – of peace and war. The speech was so prescient that, reading it today, it is difficult to see how MPs in the Chamber that day could fail to see the road to peace they were being offered. But for many it was just Old Winston, living in the past, always on the lookout for another battle to fight against modernity and progress.

He was a realist, not an alarmist, Churchill said: 'I do not believe in the imminence of war in Europe. I believe that with wisdom and with skill we may never see it in our time.' But he laid out what needed to be done – and foretold with almost uncanny accuracy what would happen if it was not done – to secure peace for the younger generation. He was no psychic, however: just facing facts that the rest of the political establishment – and Baldwin more than anyone – would ignore for as long possible.

What Churchill had learned about Germany in the summer of 1932 had turned his world – and his optimism about world peace – upside down. Germany's militaristic culture had reasserted itself, and Churchill saw German agitation

to lift the Versailles Treaty ban on its
rearmament as more than a modest request
for self-protection. What he had once called
the 'terrible engine' was gearing up again,
and Churchill understood how much more
terrible it might become this time round.

This was not just about Adolf Hitler. True,
Hitler's NSDAP was, at this point, the largest
of several right-wing parties vying to ally
themselves with this new mood, but its vote
had just fallen in the latest election. In a world
ravaged by the economic crash of 1929, the
German people were divided – but still less
than half of the electorate was attracted by the
right-wing parties promising to repudiate the
Versailles Treaty, restore German pride and
punish internal 'enemies of the people'.

Churchill warned that Britain must lead the international community to foil
the triumph of German militarism. Only seven years younger than Baldwin, he
rejected Baldwin's complacent 'old man' apathy with a radical plan: there was still
time to secure peace but it must not be wasted 'haggling about cannons, tanks,
aeroplanes and submarines,' at the Disarmament Conference.

'I have the greatest respect and admiration for the Germans and the greatest
desire that we should live on terms of good feeling and fruitful relations,' Churchill
said, 'But currently her parliamentary system was 'in abeyance … military men are
in control of the essentials.'

And while many were blaming France for not disarming, he would not: 'France
does not speak for herself alone when she speaks at Geneva,' he said, naming
Belgium, Poland, Romania, Czechoslovakia and Yugoslavia among the states who
relied on the French Army for their protection, 'as small nations before the War
used to look to the British Navy in the days of its power.'

OPPOSITE: Brownshirted SA stormtroopers show an almost religious devotion to Hitler – but 1934's
'Night of the Long Knives' would see many of their leaders killed by his SS Blackshirts.
ABOVE: This anti-Nazi poster depicting 'The True Meaning of the Hitler Salute' shows Hitler taking
money from big business. 'Millions stand behind me' says one of the smaller captions.

'Do not delude yourselves,' he told MPs. 'All these bands of sturdy Teutonic youths, marching along the streets and roads of Germany, with the light in their eyes of desire to suffer for their Fatherland, are not looking for status,' said Churchill, 'They are looking for weapons.' And – 'believe me,' he said – once they had them, they would demand restoration of lost territories and 'shake and possibly shatter to their foundations every one of the countries I have mentioned, and some other countries I have not mentioned.'

Churchill now offered a 'general principle which I humbly submit to the Government and the House, and which I earnestly trust they will ponder.'

> The removal of the just grievances of the vanquished ought to precede the disarmament of the victors. I hope I have made that quite clear.
> To bring about anything like equality of armaments, if it were in our power to do so, which it happily is not, while those grievances remain un-redressed, would be almost to appoint the day for another European war.
> To fix it as if it were a prize fight.

Now, while the victor nations of the Great War still had unchallengeable military dominance, was the time to resolve peacefully the delicate international disputes in the Balkans and the Danzig Corridor – once German, now Polish. Settle them, 'in cold blood and in a calm atmosphere', or 'drift on, inch by inch and stage by stage' until armed camps, equally matched, fought over them.

He could not recall any time in his three decades in politics, Churchill said, when the gap had been wider between the 'words which statesmen use and what is actually happening', and he urged his colleagues to 'Tell the truth to the British people. They are a tough people, a robust people.' France and her associates could defend themselves with no help from Britain, 'until or unless Germany is re-armed,' he said and, 'though I may shock the House … I would rather see another ten years or 20 years of one-sided armed peace than see a war between equally well-matched Powers or combinations of Powers – and that may be the choice.'

In conclusion, he attacked Baldwin's speech from two weeks earlier, which had created 'anxiety' in its hearers and displayed 'fatalism … perhaps helplessness' in the speaker. This was dereliction of duty: 'The responsibility of Ministers to guarantee the safety of the country from day to day, and from hour to hour, is direct and inalienable,' Churchill said. Not simply to try to prevent war in a well-meaning way but to ensure that 'the King's Dominions can be effectively defended, and will be

able to preserve, if they desire to do so, that strong and unassailable neutrality from which we must never be drawn except by the heart and conscience of the nation.'

When Churchill spoke to the House of Commons in November 1932, Germany's politics were still on a knife-edge between powerful left- and right-wing factions. The Reichstag (Imperial Parliament) had failed to produce any workable coalition that could agree on a shared solution to the country's financial problems and a joint choice for Chancellor.

President Hindenburg was therefore ruling the country by personal decree. Then, in January 1933, despite misgivings, Hindenburg appointed Hitler Chancellor and called new elections for March. In the run-up to this election the Reichstag building was burned down – apparently by Communists – and Hitler won almost half of the seats. The Reichstag now voted him total authority, temporarily, to deal with the political crisis.

Three months later, in June 1933, Welsh journalist Gareth Jones reported from Berlin that Hitler's Brownshirts were now 'masters of Germany', parading with military music through streets bedecked with Nazi flags ('pronounced Natsis', he told his British readers) as enthusiastic crowds threw out their right hands and cried 'Heil Hitler'. All other parties had been banned and their assets seized, socialistic

ABOVE: President Hindenburg (flanked by Hitler and Göring) appointed Hitler Chancellor early in 1933; when the President died in 1934, Hitler became 'Führer', uniting both roles.

books burned in midnight bonfires. Many tens of thousands of Germans were now in prison or concentration camps for their political views; Jews were deprived of their rights. Nazis had also put themselves at the head of universities, schools, boards of directors, factories, committees – every position of trust.

In the October 1933 election, the Nazi Party won 661 seats out of 661, with 95.3 per cent of the vote. A referendum on the same day confirmed 95.1 per cent of the electorate wanted to withdraw from the League of Nations.

On the day of that election, Churchill told a veterans' lunch that it was time to abandon the idea of the democratic nations disarming themselves and go straight to the collective security that had been the great promise of the League of Nations. 'You have heard me described as a warmonger,' he said, 'That is a lie.' It was a lie he would now hear on a daily basis for almost six years.

Winston Churchill would face dismissiveness and scorn for his calls for Britain to arm to defend itself while also acting through the League of Nations to curb Hitler's ambitions. But at the same time he became a magnet for those who knew he was right about Germany's military renaissance and the woeful state of Britain's defences. Isolated in Parliament, with only a few Conservative MPs, such as Brendan Bracken, Harold Macmillan and, later, Anthony Eden, to support him, he worked to gather information and build alliances across party lines, hosting a wide range of visitors at Chartwell including refugees, old political enemies, and even the Soviet ambassador Ivan Maisky.

Some people say 'Put your trust in the League of Nations,' said Churchill in 1935; others say 'Put your trust in British rearmament'. He said he wanted both. As the League of Nations gave way time and again, he would have been delighted to be proved wrong about either the power and intent of German rearmament under Hitler, or the weakness of British rearmament in response. But he was not.

Clementine's distant cousin, journalist Shiela Grant Duff, sent Winston inside information from Prague, one of many informants abroad; at home, more than 20 civil servants privately leaked vital information to Churchill through what he called 'the gathering storm'. Desmond Morton, head of the discreetly named Industrial Intelligence Centre, would quietly walk across the fields from his home just a mile away from Chartwell to ensure that Churchill had every detail on the rebuilding of the Luftwaffe. Ralph Wigram at the Foreign Office, supported by his wife Ava, passed secret files to Churchill until 1936, when he died aged just 46.

That year, Hitler took the opportunity of the Spanish Civil War to test out his new airforce (as did Mussolini) in support of the Franco rebellion, developing

what the Germans would call *Blitzkrieg* ('lightning war'), with the Basque town of Guernica the first victim. He also marched his armies back into the Rhineland in contravention of the Versailles Treaty. Churchill argued there was yet still time to save the German people – against whom he had no quarrel. 'Under the brazen surface of the totalitarian State,' he said, 'there stir and seethe all the emotions of a great, cultured, educated and once free community.' But while Hitler was being handed victory after victory without a fight or sanction by the international community, there was also the German who would think 'here is the Führer, the great leader of the country, who has raised his country so high …' This is the German for whom appeasement was just an invitation to admire the Führer more.

ABOVE: German and Italian air raids in support of a right-wing coup in Spain awoke the Left to Hitler's wider ambitions and persuaded many to support Churchill's call to rearm.

That same year of 1936, Diana Mitford married Oswald Mosley, who had travelled through the Conservative and Labour Parties before forming his own New Party and then the British Union of Fascists. The polarisation of politics in Britain in the 1930s was nowhere more clearly demonstrated than among the granddaughters of Bertie Mitford, Clementine's uncle (or possibly even father). Diana's sisters ranged politically from Communist Jessica Mitford, who went to Spain during the Civil War, to the fanatical Hitler-worshipper Unity Mitford. In a London where society ladies could wear swastika charms on their bracelets, people the Churchills had once entertained now cut them in the street. But supporters of his stance against appeasement included old friend Violet Asquith (now Lady Violet Bonham Carter), who said they had to do more than point the finger at Hitler: 'We have "pointed the finger at Mussolini" – & it has done him no harm.' She became, like TUC general secretary Walter Citrine, and former editor of *The Times* Wickham Steed, a senior member of Churchill's Anti-Nazi Council.

Also in 1936, Stanley Baldwin, now heading the National Government, told a colleague he had thought up some words to say in the Commons one day – not a speech, just a throwaway remark. About how the fairies who gathered at Winston's birth had queued up to gift him with imagination, eloquence, industry and ability. Until one fairy, protesting that no one had the right to so many gifts, had shaken the judgment and wisdom right out of him. Which was why, Baldwin would say, 'while we delight to listen to him in this House we do not take his advice.'

BELOW: Celebrating George V's Jubilee in 1935, the 'little princesses' (in pink) stand by their uncle, the future Edward VIII. Their parents stand just behind them.

Churchill's quixotic defence of Edward VIII during the Abdication Crisis that year only compounded his reputation as an eccentric out of tune with the times. His own instinctive reaction had been to assume that there was no reason King Edward VIII should not be allowed to continue his relationship with Wallis Simpson – his 'cutie'. But when in December he stood up to speak in the King's defence, he was howled down and, unable to complete his speech, left 'miserable beyond belief', said Brendan Bracken, fearful of the damage done, to the detriment of more serious issues, to his credibility.

In 1937, behind closed doors, Hitler told his military commanders he wanted *Lebensraum*, ('living room') for Germans. He also needed small wars to help stimulate the struggling German economy. In 1938 the *Anschluss* ('joining' or 'connection') brought Austria into the Greater Germany. Czechoslovakia followed in two bites.

The first was the largely German-speaking Sudetenland, whose annexation Neville Chamberlain flew to Munich to discuss with Hitler and the French Prime Minister. Returning on 29th September 1938 with a piece of paper signed by all three, Chamberlain was greeted as the hero who had delivered 'Peace in Our Time'. So long, that was, as Hitler proved a man of his word and that uniting with these other Germans was the limit of his ambition. But he wasn't, it wasn't and the rest of Czechoslovakia was swallowed up the following spring.

The Danzig Corridor, the area of dispute between Germany and Poland that Churchill had identified in 1932 as needing quick, peaceful resolution, was now contested by armies. Britain and France offered Poland guarantees – but on 1st September Hitler invaded the country. Two days later, at 11.15am, Neville Chamberlain spoke to Britain on the BBC.

The British Ambassador, Chamberlain said, had handed the German Government a note with an 11 o'clock deadline asking for an undertaking to withdraw its troops.

I have to tell you now that no such undertaking has been received, and that consequently this country is at war with Germany.

By mistake, an air raid warning was set off and people across Britain heard its wail for the first time in wartime. For Churchill, it signalled a return to Government. Chamberlain had appointed him First Lord of the Admiralty. Winston was back.

PART FOUR

1940–41

CHAPTER 11

'Never surrender'

Back in 1933, exchanging letters about India, Lord Linlithgow had laughed at Winston's conviction that it was everyone else that was 'twenty years behind the times.' 'Forgive me,' he wrote to his friend, 'in fun as well as seriousness.' It was 'rather you who are hanging, hairy, from a branch, while you splutter the atavistic shibboleths of an age destined by some to retreat into the forgotten past.' He beseeched Winston, 'as one Tory to another', to realise his mistake, 'lest irretrievably you miss the bus.'

In April 1940, Neville Chamberlain declared that it was Hitler who had 'missed the bus'. The seven months since Britain and France had declared war on Germany had been so devoid of substantial military activity in the West that the American press called it the 'phoney war'. Poland, for whose sovereignty the Allies had gone to war, had been overrun with scarcely any support, carved up between Hitler and his sudden Soviet friend Josef Stalin. Their Nazi-Soviet non-aggression pact had been signed less than two weeks before the start of the war.

Chamberlain, wanting to reassure his party that, here in the West at least, all was now well, confessed that France and Britain had been underprepared when

OPPOSITE: Huge responsibilities fell on Churchill once he became Prime Minister. The sinking of the French fleet at Oran, here being hailed as a necessary move by the whole House, weighed heavily on him personally.

they first declared war; Germany might have caused them some problems if Herr Hitler had seized his moment then. Happily, Herr Hitler's moment was past.

Within the week, the Führer had invaded neutral Denmark and Norway by land, sea and air. Denmark was unrecoverable and the Allies' attempt to counter the invasion in Norway was failing. Lack of foresight, poor planning and execution, and lack of co-ordination between Army and Navy were all blamed – public anger all the greater for the confidence that had been issuing from the Government.

The passionate House of Commons debate on 7th and 8th May 1940 in the wake of the Norway debacle has been viewed as Parliamentary democracy's finest hour, ushering in Churchill's epoch-making leadership at the precise moment it was needed. As it did – but the process was infinitely more drawn out and precarious up close than it might seem with the distance of history.

Labour leader Clement Attlee pulled no punches in the debate. It was not just Norway: 'Norway follows Czechoslovakia and Poland. Everywhere the story is "Too late."' Those mainly responsible had, he said, 'an almost uninterrupted career of failure … to win the war, we want different people at the helm.' Just as devastating for Chamberlain, from his own back benches Leo Amery attacked in the famous words of Oliver Cromwell: 'You have sat too long here for any good you have been doing. Depart, I say, and have done with you. In the name of God, go.' At the vote, Chamberlain's majority of 213 fell to 81.

Chamberlain was willing to resign, if necessary, to secure a truly National Government; he hoped Foreign Secretary Lord Halifax would succeed him – if not, it must be Winston. He sounded out both men the next day, saying he would serve under either. Churchill's one schoolboy success had been in fencing, winning the school cup: 'absolutely untouched in the finals,' he wrote at the time. He knew when to strike; when to wait his opponent out. 'Usually I talk a great deal,' he recalled, 'but on this occasion I was silent.' After a considerable pause, Halifax proceeded to talk himself out of the job. Halifax could only speak from the red benches of the Lords; Winston must speak for the Government among the green benches of the Commons. Halifax wrote later that, even if he had taken on the job of Prime Minister, he would have been 'a more or less honorary Prime Minister, living in a kind of twilight just outside the things that really mattered.' Chamberlain 'reluctantly', wrote Halifax, 'and Churchill evidently with much less reluctance,' accepted his view.

Churchill had won the final – or so he thought. However, Chamberlain was not yet convinced he must go. The crucial question was would Labour serve under Chamberlain after all? He now consulted Attlee, who said it was for the Party's National Executive Committee, assembling in Bournemouth for the Party Conference, to decide; he was taking the train there tomorrow.

Then, everything changed.

At dawn, Hitler's Luftwaffe and Panzer divisions invaded the Low Countries. By seven o'clock the Belgian and Dutch Ambassadors delivered requests for assistance to Lord Halifax at the Foreign Office. Churchill held an early breakfast at the Admiralty with his Army and RAF opposite numbers. In Downing Street,

ABOVE: Like many young officers, Randolph Churchill married in haste at the start of the war. His wife Pamela (née Digby) became a trusted member of his father's circle.

Chamberlain decided it was his duty to stay: 'The next three or four days' battle will determine the fate of civilisation for the next one hundred years.' He still had the overwhelming support of his own party and had also secured the Liberals. But Labour, commanding a quarter of the House, was vital.

As Chamberlain and Halifax lunched with their wives at the Dorchester, Attlee and his deputy Arthur Greenwood took the train to Bournemouth. That afternoon Chamberlain, handed a phone message during yet another meeting, read it silently and waited until the end before bringing up an 'additional' item: he was leaving for the Palace. Labour's National Executive Committee had been united: it would never join a Chamberlain coalition but under a new Prime Minister would 'take its share of responsibility'.

Arriving back at Waterloo, Attlee and Greenwood were met by a naval attaché: Mr Chamberlain would broadcast to the nation after the nine o'clock news – and Prime Minister Churchill was waiting for them in the Admiralty Board Room. Here, beneath a full-length portrait of Nelson, Churchill laid out his plan for a five-man War Cabinet: the three of them plus Halifax, who stayed as foreign secretary, and Chamberlain, who still commanded the loyalty of most of the Conservative majority and would be Lord President of the Council.

Churchill promised Attlee a third of the remaining ministerial posts for Labour, but also wanted union leader Ernie Bevin, his old adversary from the General Strike, as his Minister for Labour and National Service – in this war, Churchill's government would call on talents wherever he found them.

Churchill also co-opted old friend Lord Beaverbrook for a job he'd just invented: Minister of Aircraft Production. 'Of course I believe in the devil,' Evelyn Waugh is supposed to have said, 'How else could I account for Lord Beaverbrook?' Churchill had been on the receiving end of the Canadian press baron's vicious press campaigns more than once, but their relationship could be no better indicated than by the fact that each let the other proofread their books. Running tight production schedules was nothing new for a newspaper proprietor and Churchill had always known the RAF would be key to Britain's survival.

This was his team; this was his task; this was his destiny. A daunting one for anyone – but a speech Churchill made on St George's Day 1933 foreshadowed his determination now: 'We ought to rejoice at the responsibilities with which destiny has honoured us, and be proud that we are guardians of our country in an age when her life is at stake.'

Many MPs on the Conservative benches saved their cheers for Chamberlain, not Churchill, as they entered, ready for the Prime Minister's maiden speech. And the words that would go down in history received a mixed reception on first hearing.

I would say to the House, as I said to those who have joined this Government: 'I have nothing to offer but blood, toil, tears and sweat' ... You ask, what is our policy? I will say: it is to wage war, by sea, land, and air, with all our might and with all the strength that God can give us: to wage war against a monstrous tyranny, never surpassed in the dark, lamentable catalogue of human crime. That is our policy. You ask, what is our aim? I can answer in one word: It is victory, victory at all costs, victory in spite of all terror, victory, however long and hard the road may be; for without victory, there is no survival.

Harold Nicolson MP was greatly moved: it was, he wrote to his wife Vita Sackville-West, 'the finest speech that I have ever heard.' Vita, hearing it on the BBC, replied: 'Even repeated by the announcer it sent shivers (not of fear) down my spine. I think that one of the reasons why one is stirred by his Elizabethan phrases is the whole massive backing of power and resolve behind them, like a great fortress: they are never words for words' sake.' London office worker Nell Carver got shivers too: 'Winston's speeches send all sorts of thrills racing up & down my veins & I feel fit to tackle the largest Hun!' she wrote in her diary, adding, 'Probably if only a small one threatened my hearth & home I should creep into a corner — but that is as it may be!'

The day after Churchill pledged victory, the French Prime Minister came on the phone: 'We are beaten; we have lost the battle.' A square mile of Rotterdam's medieval heart had been flattened by bombs, in preparation for the tanks to roll in — the Dutch had capitulated. More than two million French soldiers in the field, along with a quarter of a million men of the British Expeditionary Force, were falling back. Churchill flew to Paris and found Prime Minister Paul Reynaud's government crippled by a defeatism, which he did all he could do with his broken French to dispel. But the Allied position was deteriorating with astonishing speed.

By the time Britain's new Prime Minister made his first BBC broadcast on Sunday 19th May, the British Expeditionary Force was trapped in a pocket around the Channel ports of Calais and Dunkirk. The radio distillation of his Commons speech went out around the world: 'in a solemn hour for the life of our country, of our Empire, of our Allies, and above all of the cause of Freedom'.

'Tell the truth to the British people,' he had urged the Government back in 1932. 'They are a tough people, a robust people.' Now he set out for them, in broad terms, the gravity of the military position, and the fight for freedom they were engaged in, not just for nation and Empire, but those 'shattered states and bludgeoned races: the Czechs, the Poles, the Norwegians, the Danes, the Dutch, the Belgians. Upon all of whom the long dark night of barbarism will descend, unbroken even by a star of hope, unless we conquer. As conquer we must. As conquer we shall.'

Over the next week, Britain's situation in France became untenable; men were retreating into the seaside town of Dunkirk while, in Westminster, Churchill faced his own battle for survival. Lord Halifax urged the War Cabinet to explore a negotiated peace, brokered by neutral Mussolini. It was the rational position. But Churchill's view was, and would remain, that the British people would, should and did choose another path, not just for their own sake but for the sake of the whole world: the path of resolute resistance. If necessary, for years. If necessary, alone. If necessary, to the death.

On Sunday 26th May, Reynaud flew to London. He had been Prime Minister just two months longer than Churchill and, while he would never conclude a separate peace, he said he might soon be replaced. Churchill seemed to waver on the idea of talks. On Monday the Luftwaffe showered Dunkirk with maps bearing the words: 'Your troops are entirely surrounded – stop fighting! Put down your arms!'

The British had been ordered to Dunkirk for evacuation. More than 7,000 men embarked that day and, as Göring's planes strafed beaches and sunk ships with apparent impunity, Churchill

was told 'Operation Dynamo' might be able to get 30,000 troops home – one man in ten. On Tuesday, he adjourned yet another War Cabinet conclave to address his new full Cabinet. If he could not rally them, it was all over. One minister recorded that Churchill exhorted them: 'If this long island story of ours is to end at last, let it end only when each one of us lies choking in his own blood upon the ground.' Their response was overwhelming; the negotiated peace option was effectively squashed.

The task now was to save as much of the BEF as possible. The BBC broadcast an appeal for volunteers, 'experienced in marine internal combustion engines' and with 'good knowledge of coastal navigation'. With the Luftwaffe screaming overhead, almost 700 ships, large and small, plied back and forth – fishing boats, lifeboats, motor yachts and paddle steamers alongside the Royal Navy – bringing home Churchill's last hope. His promise of 30,000 men was met, then surpassed, as day by day the

OPPOSITE: Officers of the Royal Ulster Rifles awaiting evacuation at Bray-Dunes near Dunkirk.
ABOVE: The images of the beaches became instantly iconic back in Britain.

tally rose. The eventual rescue, over nine days, of a third of a million men, including many French and Belgians, was not christened the 'Miracle of Dunkirk' for nothing.

The last man embarked, just before the Germans occupied the town, in the early hours of Tuesday 4th June. That afternoon Churchill warned the House of Commons: 'Wars are not won by evacuations. But there was a victory inside this deliverance …'

> I have, myself, full confidence that, if all do their duty, if nothing is neglected, and if the best arrangements are made, as they are being made, we shall prove ourselves once again able to defend our island home, to ride out the storm of war, and to outlive the menace of tyranny, if necessary for years, if necessary alone. At any rate, that is what we are going to try to do … we shall not flag or fail. We shall go on to the end, we shall fight in France, we shall fight on the seas and oceans, we shall fight with growing confidence and growing strength in the air, we shall defend our island, whatever the cost may be. We shall fight on the beaches, we shall fight on the landing grounds, we shall fight in the fields and in the streets, we shall fight in the hills; we shall never surrender.

The Ministry of Information hastily memoed the BBC to omit the words 'if necessary alone' from the extract read on the News, lest it give the impression Britain believed the French would give up the fight. The following evening, in a broadcast on the BBC, the novelist J.B. Priestley asked, 'Doesn't it seem to you to have an inevitable air about it – as if we had turned a page in the history of Britain and seen a chapter headed "Dunkirk" – and perhaps seen too a picture of the troops on the beach waiting to embark?'

In the first week of Churchill's premiership, one and a half million men had answered the call for Local Defence Volunteers (which Winston soon renamed the Home Guard). Writer George Orwell, a veteran of the Spanish Civil War, now instinctively sized up familiar streets in London's West End for possible machine-gun nests – though they had, as yet, no guns of any kind. He thought the Government might be nervous of arming the people; in fact it had no guns to give them. Men had returned from Dunkirk with little more than the uniforms they stood up in. And Britain – from Land's End to John O'Groats – contained barely 500 field guns and only 200 tanks.

OPPOSITE: The *Massey Shaw*, one of the 'little ships' welcomed back to the Thames after Dunkirk, was a London Fire Brigade fireboat – which went on to do sterling work during the Blitz.

And still the Allied cause was everywhere in retreat. Reluctantly, Churchill evacuated troops from Norway. On the day Norway capitulated, Mussolini declared war alongside Germany. The Luftwaffe bombed the Paris suburbs and on 14th June, German tanks rolled along the Champs-Élysées. By phone and in person, Churchill pledged the fleeing French Government air support the RAF could ill afford – he even offered to unite the two nations so they could fight on as one. But General Pétain, taking over from Reynaud, made peace with Germany. Pétain now ruled the south and the French colonies from Vichy; Germany occupied northern France, Paris and the whole Atlantic coast – completing a Nazi seaboard against Britain from the Arctic Circle to the Spanish border.

CHAPTER 12

'Finest hour'

'The battle of France is over,' Churchill told the nation, once French capitulation seemed certain: 'I expect the Battle of Britain is about to begin … Let us therefore brace ourselves to our duties, and so bear ourselves that, if the British Empire and its Commonwealth last for a thousand years, men will still say, "This was their finest hour."'

It is doubtful, when he spoke the words, that Churchill thought the 'Battle of Britain' would enter the history books as purely an aerial battle. Across the Channel, Hitler was planning for a full invasion by air, sea and land, and that was what Churchill was bracing the nation to receive.

Two of the Prime Minister's peacetime secretaries give insight into how the Prime Minister's speeches now worked in wartime. 'He makes you feel as though you were sharing his work and this is very satisfying to the ego,' wrote the first. 'I've never heard anyone describe it so well,' said the second: 'He did make you feel as though you were part of the work, and were sharing in it. You weren't just a cog in a great wheel – you were going with him.' In British democracy's greatest – perhaps its final – battle, Winston Churchill was preparing to be magnificent, and with that ability to make people feel they were 'sharing his work', he readied his audience for the task of being magnificent too.

The 'Dunkirk spirit', though not yet described as such, was making itself felt for the first time. It had not been much in evidence on the beaches themselves. There had been courage, and discipline, but it had been a defeat as anguished and desperate as any, and soldiers had been astonished to find themselves greeted as heroes as they arrived in England. But they, the Royal Navy that brought them home, and above all the instantly famous little ships, were a new chapter in the long tale of British history. How had we ever won, many asked, *unless* as the underdog and by the skin

OPPOSITE: Caught in this air raid on Ramsgate, on his train back to London Churchill devised a wartime insurance scheme that spread the cost of property losses in the Blitz across the nation as a whole.

of our teeth? Bravely, beset by blunders and preferably with a wry joke or two along the way: Agincourt, the Armada, Trafalgar, Waterloo … The backs-to-the-wall legend – true or not – was a vital weapon in Britain's almost empty armoury.

In this war, Churchill the master storyteller would narrate his listeners' own lives back to them in terms of the 'Island Story' they had learned at school. In the 'Finest Hour' speech, he took them back to 'the moment we declared war on September 3rd' (some listeners would relive their emotions when they heard the air raid sirens, before they discovered it was a silly mistake); back to the dreadful litany of defeats in the last war – before the final victory. It might be helpful, Churchill said, for 'every man and woman' to think of the famous lines when facing what lay ahead:

> He nothing common did or mean
> Upon that memorable scene.

That scene, as no one schooled around the Empire needed reminding, was the death scene of Charles I, who wore two shirts on the day of his execution lest he shiver and the people think he was frightened. How did Churchill think this would help 'every man and woman'? Perhaps he was hinting at the phrase that he was careful to avoid using in his speeches – except once, in secret session of the House of Commons on 20th June 1940, where it could be delivered without derision and which we know about only from his idiosyncratic prompt notes: 'This supreme battle depends upon the courage of the ordinary man and woman. Whatever happens, keep a stiff upper lip.'

Certainly, the day France signed peace terms with Germany, American journalist Raymond Daniell was puzzled to find Londoners suddenly rather buoyant. He asked his ancient taxi driver if he seriously thought Britain could beat Hitler alone. 'Well, we can't if we don't try, can we, Guv'nor?' came the laconic reply. At his office, the lift operator observed: 'Things are looking better, aren't they, sir … there's nobody left to desert us now.' England was, as another young man put it, 'in the final now'.

In July, Churchill spoke on the BBC of this war that was the 'War of the Unknown Warriors'. Every village, town and city would be defended, he said, while, 'The vast mass of London itself, fought street by street, could easily devour an entire hostile army; and we would rather see London laid in ruins and ashes than that it should be tamely and abjectly enslaved.'

The Prime Minister was a good 'puller-up of socks', Canadian firewoman Yvonne Green wrote home, to a mother she would not live to see again.

TOGETHER

London is the best place to be in. There is nowt one can do about it now. Anyway my blood is up and I'm dying to have a poke at the Germans. If one has the mischance to land in the garden, he's going to have a hot time before I'm through with him. I'm glad to be Johnny-on-the-spot with a chance of taking a crack at them complete with saucepans of boiling water aimed with great precision from the kitchen window.

Churchill's skilled, long-practised weaving of past, present and future resonated across many divides that had once seemed important. Leslie Paul, founder of the Woodcraft Folk youth movement, shared few political opinions with his Prime Minister but, hearing him, felt that: 'Churchill's voice is that of an aggressive old man of the tribe defending his cave home from wolves. The voice of a man who knows he has to win or there will be no tribe.'

It was now a tribe of bewildering complexity. Britain was home in 1940 to Imperial expats rallying to the Mother Country, plus refugees, royals and governments-in-exile from those 'shattered states and bludgeoned races' of Europe. Writing to a friend, child welfare officer Isabelle Granger said he 'would not mind London at all now':

Everywhere are red, apple-faced New Zealanders, Australians (they are all so fruit-like, I cannot think why), and Polish airmen, and French soldiers in kepis, and flowing cloaks and Czechs and Norwegians in their greenish-grey uniforms – all sorts of languages and uniforms: the red bobs of the French sailors' caps come jogging cheerfully along the Strand.

ABOVE: Wartime posters reminded people in Britain that they were supported by troops from all around the Empire, fighting together as one.

Australian Bert Snow, holidaying in London when war broke out, joined the city's auxiliary ambulance service; Jamaican Fernando Henriques and Trinidadian George A. Roberts went for its fire service; Nigerian E.I. Epkenyon was an air raid warden in the West End. The station master at Leicester Square felt honoured to witness a heavyweight bout between a Canadian military policeman and a fellow countryman who refused to leave his station platform ('it went through my mind that they were probably lumberjacks in their own country'). Meanwhile in Cornwall, three Muslim transport companies of the Royal Indian Army Service Corps, rescued from the beaches of Dunkirk, awaited specialist training in the mountains of Wales.

Hitler hadn't expected to have to invade Britain to get a peace deal but now he was drawing up a plan. On 16th July, Hitler's *Unternehmen Seelöwe* ('Operation Sealion') was agreed. First on the agenda: the RAF must be so 'beaten down in its morale and in fact, that it can no longer display any appreciable aggressive force in opposition to the German crossing.'

The RAF was its own League of Nations. Fifteen nationalities, predominantly Poles and Czechs, flew alongside home-grown crews to defend Britain's ports and convoys, factories and airfields. One squadron of Spitfires was paid for by Basutoland; the Boy Scouts of the West Indies were collecting second-hand binoculars and telescopes to send to the Observer Corps …

As the 'Battle of Britain' progressed, Luftwaffe bombers, guided by radio beams, were able to fly by night as well as by day and a fighter had to scour a sector of night sky stretching several miles in all directions to intercept them. Yet, as summer slipped away, Göring's delivery of a 'beaten down' RAF was falling overdue.

'The hour has come when one or other of us will crumble, and that one will not be National Socialist Germany.'

Beaverbrook's spectacular progress in Spitfire and Hurricane production meant another 'crate' awaiting whenever a pilot bailed out or ditched at sea. But Churchill knew just how few pilots Britain had to rely on – on 19th August Fighter Command shortened its training period from six months to just two weeks. Then, five days later, a night raid bombed a slew of London suburbs and scored a bullseye on the City of London's square mile.

Churchill, aware the Führer had reserved for himself the decision of bombing the capital, ordered retaliation on Berlin. But had Hitler really ordered the bombing of London? Or was it, as had been argued since, pilot error? If so, it was a mistake that changed history. In Berlin, the Führer promised a furious response to 'Mr Churchill' and 'the aerial night attacks he has concocted'. If Britain attacked German cities, its own would be razed to the ground: 'We will stop the handiwork of those night-pirates, so help us God! The hour will come when one or the other of us will crumble, and that one will not be National Socialist Germany.'

••• ——————— •••

'The whole bloody world's on fire!' came the call from the docks on Saturday 7th September, as the capital experienced its very own lightning war: the 'London Blitz' had begun. Over four days and nights, bombs rained on London from the East End to Buckingham Palace. At the same time, via neutral Sweden and America, Hitler offered Britain's Foreign Secretary his peace terms: the world would be divided into two economic spheres: the 'continental' run by Germany; the 'maritime and colonial' by Britain and the USA.

After four days, Lord Halifax gave Hitler Britain's answer: it had not entered the war in self-defence but to defend the freedom and independence of other states, thus it was now for Germany to prove, by 'deeds not words', its willingness to restore them. The 'indiscriminate bombing of London without the slightest relation to military objectives,' he said, had only strengthened British resolve.

So legendary has 'The Blitz' chapter of the Island Story become – and Winston Churchill's part in it – that debunking it has produced its own literature. Not everyone behaved as perfectly as the legend has it, shocked modern authors reveal; not everyone thought Churchill was perfect. To which puzzled Blitzed citizens might well respond: 'Well, yes – don't you read the papers?'

Did some people despair to the point of suicide? Yes. Did some people go mad with grief? Yes. Did some people betray their fellow countrymen in all the mean, small peacetime ways of thieves and con-men and petty selfishness and gross cruelty? Yes. It was all there in the court and coroners' reports. The press was not completely free: the Communist *Daily Worker* had been banned at the start of the war and 'D-notices' prevented military intelligence leaks – while a British censor sat with their finger on the pause button during live broadcasts by foreign journalists, just in case. But sceptical American journalists who came to correct the over-romanticised scenario being reported in the press by seeing what it was 'really' like, found it was pretty much as their colleagues had been reporting all along.

Everyone in Britain knew that the attitude of neutral America was vitally important; everyone in America was alive to the danger of propaganda. US newsman Raymond Daniell was dismayed to discover many of his readers at home believed they were getting fake news – stories written by American journalists but then, 'tossed in a hopper where … men bent on suppressing the truth and getting the United States into the war rewrote them.' As a city he had grown to love was smashed to bits from the air, 'It was impossible to be neutral in thought,' he wrote, but 'journalistic integrity is quite another matter.'

As for Churchill being perfect, while some of those closest to him in this great task confessed 'you can't help but love him,' others – beset by the constant stream of memos, ideas and exhortations that flowed from the typewriters of his secretaries – confided to their diaries that the sooner the Old Man dropped dead and let them get on with their job the better.

For four decades, Churchill had presented a challenge for successive Prime Ministers: how to harness his prodigious energies and abilities while curbing his capacity to make wrong – sometimes very wrong – decisions. Now that challenge had fallen upon … Winston himself. He found it no easier: writing to his son that, while Beaverbrook 'fights everybody and resigns every day … I have to restrain my natural pugnacity by sitting on my own head. How bloody!'

The necessity of doing so had been borne in on him by Clemmie. She made a point of cheering and consoling those Cabinet and military colleagues that her husband's abrasiveness might have offended. Many who found him sarcastic and overbearing, impatient of others' ideas, appealed to her and found not only

a sympathetic ear but a champion. 'My Darling Winston,' she wrote,

> I must confess that I have noticed a deterioration in your manner. I cannot bear that those who serve the Country & yourself should not love you as well as admire and respect you – Besides you won't get the best results by irascibility & rudeness. They will breed either dislike or a slave mentality . . . please forgive your loving devoted & watchful
> Clemmie.

Some wrong, or deeply questionable, decisions would follow in the Total War to which Winston now committed himself heart and soul, as he acknowledged to MPs: 'I have never ventured to predict the future. I stand by my original programme, blood, toil, tears, and sweat, which is all I ever offered, to which I added five months later, "many shortcomings, mistakes and disappointments."'

IF YOU ARE BOMBED OUT
and have no friends to go to

ask a
POLICEMAN
or your **WARDEN**
where to find your
REST CENTRE

ISSUED BY THE MINISTRY OF HEALTH

He was only human after all, leading other humans, in a superhuman struggle. One who chose to share – and this was what made Churchill in 1940 remarkable – his human hopes and fears, his strengths and weaknesses, as frankly as was possible with millions of his fellow humans across Britain and the Empire. 'Everybody is reading Churchill's speech', wrote one London woman. 'What a superb phrase-maker he is – death and sorrow the companions of our journey, hardship our garment – that is worthy of Milton or Burke or the Authorised Version itself.'

'Trust the people' had been his father's political watchword; Winston had stuck to it throughout the ups and downs of his career – and he stuck to it now, showing more faith than many in his administration, in the people who would not let the side down.

OPPOSITE: Churchill inspects damage with the King and Queen. The raids on Buckingham Palace bound London together and were a huge propaganda blunder for Germany.
ABOVE: On the Home Front, the expectation was that everyone had a common-sense duty to help everyone else, with the local bobby and air raid warden available in a crisis.

Cockney bricklayer Bill Regan now worked in 'Heavy Rescue': tunnelling through bombed buildings to extricate the living and dead, filling bushel baskets with human remains. In that first week, he and his wife Vi experienced bombs coming 'close, closer and we both thought curtains' in their damp back-garden Anderson shelter.

'Landscape rearranged, and beginning to look like Spain and Poland,' he recorded (Bill, a fan of Samuel Pepys' diary, had started taking notes himself). Later that week, he arrived home to a rope blocking off his street. Vi was sweeping fallen plaster into the road outside their house: an unexploded bomb had fallen opposite.

> She showed me [the] hole where the U.X.B. had gone, and wasn't concerned about it. Warden Herbie Martin had tried to persuade her, and her Mum and Dad, to take shelter in Saunders Ness school but they declined. Vi said she wasn't afraid of dying, provided she didn't have a lingering death. Surprisingly, this took away the worry I had at the back of my mind while on duty.

Bill also noted the parrot rescued in a squashed cage that squawked 'F— Hitler, F— Hitler, F— Hitler,' ('my sentiments exactly'); the lorry carrying an anti-aircraft gun that shot in one street, then another. 'Then back again "ditto repeato", to cheer us up or confuse the enemy. Anyhow, it's one of Churchill's better ideas.' He also noted, after the early days, that he was seeing more bombs than casualties: 'It's becoming expensive to kill English people.'

Winston Churchill had noticed the same thing, as air raid warden Barbara Nixon heard him explain in what she called a 'risky' broadcast after the Blitz had been raging for a month. The casualty rate, the Prime Minister said, while grievous, was a fraction of what had been expected before the war. And, since so many bombs fell on already-ruined buildings, the law of diminishing returns meant it would take Hitler ten more years to flatten even half of London. (After which, he said, 'progress would be much slower'.) Barbara found her neighbours, in the firing line most nights, 'cheered and amused' – 'Fancy the ol' man thinking up that one!'

On the first Blitz weekend, Air Vice-Marshal Keith Park had flown over London and said, 'Thank God for that.' Horrible as it was, bombs that were falling on

OPPOSITE: In September 1940, the Battle of Britain was being fought out beneath Churchill's eyes at Uxbridge (above); within six months it was a neatly packaged episode for history (below), and, through Churchill's speeches, already passing into legend.

London could not also be falling on fighter stations that were at the end of their tether. The following weekend, on Sunday 15th September, he was with the Prime Minister in the Operations Room at Group HQ No. 11 in Uxbridge, watching what might be the final, losing action of the air battle develop on a huge map below them.

Green blips on a screen at a coastal radar station miles away appeared as a coloured tiddly-wink on a map in the Filter Room, then an arrow. Via headphones worn by girls in the Ops Room, these became the path of the Luftwaffe on their own map, allowing Park, looking down with Churchill, to judge which squadron to scramble next. The system was miraculous; the message ominous. Either side of noon, in two waves, Göring despatched more than 500 planes towards London to tempt up the last RAF fighters and sweep them from the skies. As panels of lights showed squadron after squadron engaged, Churchill asked what further reserves could be called into play and, Park wrote, 'looked grave' when told there were none. 'Well I might,' Winston responded later. 'The odds were great; the margins small; the stakes infinite.'

But on that Sunday, 15th September, later named 'Battle of Britain Day', the RAF had shot down two German planes for every one lost. The raiders had been literally decimated – one German plane in ten downed. Two days later, Hitler postponed *Seelöwe* indefinitely.

'The Battle of Britain' was almost over – for the purposes of the history books, at least. Quite literally: *The Battle of Britain: August–October 1940*, published the following March, price sixpence or 50 copies for one pound, sold 300,000 copies in its first week. Written by Hilary Saunders MC, it was the first of a series of Ministry of Information paperbacks in which the long years of war would be

BETTER POT-LUCK with Churchill today **THAN HUMBLE PIE** under Hitler tomorrow **DON'T WASTE FOOD!**

instantly packaged for those fighting it, bringing coherence to an open-ended and unpredictable conflict. The Blitz would be packaged in its turn.

The British had confidence that they would win 'in the end': Dunkirk, the Battle of Britain, and now the Blitz, would be the first chapters in the story of how they won. That the British already saw these three opening chapters as three triumphs was mystifying to the German High Command. In modern terms it would be called 'controlling the narrative'. Not only had Churchill delivered Britain – and the world – a famous British victory in the Battle of Britain, he had made at least some Londoners laugh, as 1940 drew to a close, at the thought of Hitler foolishly wasting his bombs on ten more years of Blitz.

Of course we know now that the 'Battle of Britain' victory was as great and pivotal as Churchill's words had made it. In London, Winston Churchill had no way of knowing, then, whether a new year would bring a 'Second Battle of Britain' – nor what the result of that battle might be. In Berlin, Adolf Hitler had not yet made up his mind on the matter. But he was starting to consider whether there might be an easier victory to be won, a more vulnerable target, elsewhere.

So much, then, for the 'Battle of Britain'. The 'Finest Hour' Churchill had spoken of in the same speech, however, was still only ticking through its opening seconds. The simplicity of the 17-word laurel wreath Churchill placed on the brows of the young heroes of the RAF on 20th August 1940 – 'Never in the field of human conflict was so much owed by so many to so few' – is remembered. What are forgotten are the 5,000 other words of that speech to the Commons: a measure of the weight and complexity of the task facing Winston each dawn. This

ABOVE: Britain was not self-sufficient in food and the Merchant Navy was vital to survival. Growing as much as possible and wasting nothing was essential.
OPPOSITE: A Caribbean merchant seaman trains with a Lewis gun. Running the gauntlet of the U-boats was a huge, perilous operation in which around one in four wartime merchant sailors died.

particular speech balanced sympathy for France with condemnation of 'the men of Vichy'. Justification for Britain's naval blockade of American aid to occupied Europe with a recognition of the role of still-neutral America in the 'long future of the British Commonwealth of Nations'.

Finally, Churchill gave the Island Story another burnish: 'The whole of the warring nations were engaged', he said, 'Not only soldiers, but the entire population, men, women and children. The fronts are everywhere.'

> If it is a case of the whole nation fighting and suffering together, that ought to suit us, because we are the most united of all the nations, because we entered the war upon the national will and with our eyes open, and because we have been nurtured in freedom and individual responsibility and are the products, not of totalitarian uniformity, but of tolerance and variety.

US General Sherman probably never actually said 'War is hell.' Churchill probably never actually capped that with 'If you're going through hell, keep going.' What he did say, though, and append to countless wartime memos, was 'KBO': Keep Buggering On.

CHAPTER 13

'The English-Speaking People'

'London's psychological situation is deteriorating daily,' Joseph Goebbels recorded in his diary as this autumn of supposed 'lightning war' dragged on. However, 'Churchill's monster is not yet on the point of collapse.' 'The English are tough,' he conceded: 'They are still holding out, after a fashion.' Cheeringly, he saw 'waves of pessimism emanating from London … We receive reports that morale in London has reached rock bottom.'

'The only thing keeping them going is the famous English stubbornness,' he wrote in one entry that might have made Winston chuckle. 'Read an essay on the English: their best weapons are their phlegm and their stupidity. In their position, any other nation would have collapsed long since.'

Reading all the newspapers in bed, as he did every morning, the Prime Minister would have seen, as 1940 drew to a close, many trailers for a series of *Daily Herald* articles on the 'Twelve Riddles of 1941': 'Will Hitler invade Britain? Will America enter the war? What are Stalin's plans?' And, good to see: 'Where do we go when we win?' They might have added a 13th: 'How will we cope with a second Great Fire of London as big as the first – only happening much faster and while being bombed at the same time?'

The raid on the night of 29th December 1940 swept away half the Square Mile, including the entire Barbican area, in one night. At its height, a firewoman at Lambeth's HQ saw her officer go white as he took a phone call. 'That was the Prime Minister,' he told her. 'He said that St Paul's must be saved at all costs.' Though grateful for the thought, the Dean wrote afterwards, when it was rung through to the clerics and architects of St Paul's Watch putting out incendiary bomb fires with buckets and stirrup pumps, 'it would not be true to say that the Watch was spurred to greater efforts, for it was already extended to the limit of human endurance.'

OPPOSITE: This photograph of Clemmie accompanying Winston on the Thames to inspect bomb damage after another night of bombing was a family favourite.

'War's Greatest Picture,' the *Daily Mail* trumpeted over the photograph that captured the cathedral emerging from clouds of smoke, the lights of the firestorm below glinting on the cross on its dome. And, indeed, it is often seen as symbolic of Britain's entire war. The picture was taken, however, almost exactly halfway through Hitler's experiment to see whether – even without tanks and troops on the ground – you could defeat a united people by bombing alone. He had already made his judgement. Though the Blitz would continue until April, on 29th December, as the City of London was being bombed, a coded message from a Berlin spy reached Moscow: 'Hitler has ordered preparations for war with the USSR.' Stalin dismissed it – he didn't believe his untrusted friend would turn on him quite so soon. But it was genuine: a few days earlier, Hitler had told his commanders to prepare, 'even before the conclusion of the war against England, to crush Soviet Russia in a rapid campaign.'

Meanwhile, as London burned, on the other side of the world Americans settled down on 29th December 1940 for one of President Roosevelt's 'Fireside Chats'. The USA would help Britain, he said, in the same way that any neighbour would lend a neighbour a fire hose if his house was on fire … It sounded sensible, and comforting, but made no specific promises.

Later, Churchill would conjure up the phrase 'Special Relationship' to contain and obscure all the complexities and contradictions arising between a rising world power and a declining empire. But the phrase works equally well for the two men: Churchill and Roosevelt, locked together by history and by telephone. And from the moment Churchill declared his implacable determination to fight on,

ABOVE: How much protection the Whitehall War Rooms bunker provided to those inside while a Blitz was on is questionable – Winston sometimes went up top to see what was going on anyway.
OPPOSITE: The close-up of St Paul's surviving the flames became iconic; this wide shot puts it in context. Widespread devastation wiped away almost half of the City of London in one night.

no political relationship mattered more. Britain's survival depended on getting America's President – and its people – to understand that they needed Britain for their own democracy to survive. And to do so before it was too late.

Winston had been hurt and disappointed, in May 1940, to learn from the Canadian Prime Minister that Roosevelt had asked him to ensure Churchill ordered the Royal Navy to Canada if Britain lost the war – but to hide the fact that the idea came from America. It had been against this background Churchill delivered the words following 'never surrender' on 4th June:

> ... and even if, which I do not for a moment believe, this island or a large part of it were subjugated and starving, then our Empire beyond the seas, armed and guarded by the British fleet, would carry on the struggle, until, in God's good time, the New World, with all its power and might, steps forth to the rescue and the liberation of the old.

However, as he pointed out sharply via an intermediary, he could not speak for any collaborationist successor – a message Roosevelt found 'alarming and distressing'. The same emotions that soon confronted Churchill and led to one of his most bitter decisions: sinking the French Fleet at Oran on 3rd July 1940 to stop it falling into enemy hands.

Roosevelt was all too aware of America's peril. Britain, despite the hammering it was getting, was a great military power; the United States, despite its huge industrial potential, was not, nor was in any sense ready for even a defensive war if forced to fight one. America, like Europe, had emerged from the horrors of the Great War with no wish to be dragged into another. It had retired behind its Atlantic moat, refusing even to join the League of Nations. Yet, once Britain fell, war might come to America's shores. Hitler would rule the waves not just in the Atlantic on its East Coast but also the in the Pacific on its West, which was now scattered with US territories. Roosevelt was advised by his Chief of Naval Operations that if it came to a war – whether against Hitler's Axis ally Japan or anyone else – 'if Britain wins decisively against Germany we could win everywhere' but that if Britain went down, 'While we might not lose everywhere, we might, possibly, not win anywhere.'

Politically, powerful American voices called for Britain to beat Hitler if it could, fine; if not, it wasn't America's problem – if it was even a problem at all. 'Perhaps

the Nazi ideal was a sounder ideal than our constitutional system,' the *New Yorker*'s E.B. White heard on the social circuit in the summer of 1940, plus 'England is really rotten', and the duty of any intelligent person was 'to remain in the role of innocent bystander.' White wrote, 'I feel sick when I find anyone adjusting his mind to the new tyranny which is succeeding abroad … If it is boyish to believe that a human being should live free, then I'll gladly arrest my development and let the rest of the world grow up.'

Writer Eric Sevareid, who had made his name exposing virulently antisemitic Silver Shirts in Minnesota, travelled to Germany before the war, to France and, after France's fall, to London. But it was not until neutral Lisbon, waiting to fly home among spies and refugees of all nations, that he decided his 'more astute colleagues' had been right all along: 'There was no possible living with Fascism, even for a strong America … Europe was small, and with Europe gone the world was very small.'

In September 1940, a British mission arrived in Washington with a precious cargo: Britain's most secret, most astonishing scientific advances. After initial doubts, Churchill had agreed to scientist Henry Tizard's idea of sharing Britain's secrets to make use of America's much greater, and more secure, manufacturing strength. Tentatively, Tizard and the American defence committee danced around what secrets each side might already know. Some aspects of British radar were matched by US knowledge, in others the Americans were way behind.

There were many areas where Britain's legacy science from the years of peace was infused with huge input from the refugee scientists from Europe, something Churchill noted gratefully in his speech paying tribute to 'The Few'. The Nazis' loss had been Britain's gain: 'Our science is definitely ahead of theirs.'

Churchill was as full of enthusiasm as ever to explore what science and technology could offer the war effort. In peace, he had fought for peace; in war he fought for the victory without which there would be no survival. He was gaining ever more insight into the mind of Hitler from the reports in buff folders arriving from Bletchley Park (thanks to a generous Polish gift of an Enigma machine in August 1939). Reports came, too – as well as actual prototypes – from the experimental unit he set up 10 miles from the Prime Minister's official country seat of Chequers, a unit soon known as 'Churchill's toyshop'.

OPPOSITE: Clementine inspects a shelter with Home Secretary Herbert Morrison. If you had no garden to put an 'Anderson' in, the 'Morrison' offered some protection if the roof fell in.

He had not been as shocked as many might have been to discover how far knowledge of nuclear technology had progressed by 1940, nor doubted that any advantages the Allies could gain over the Axis on that front would be vital. These secrets, too, had gone in the locked metal deed box in Henry Tizard's luggage, alongside plans for Frank Whittle's jet engine and a host of other innovations.

In the US Presidential election of November 1940, both of the main candidates stood behind the logic of supplying what both referred to as 'aid' to Britain (although, under US law, all military supplies had to be bought and paid for before they left America's shores). 'If Britain fails,' said Republican Wendell Willkie, 'we are utterly, and savagely, alone. Almost no nation on earth, except Britain, owes us anything but disillusionment and ill-will … We must send and we must keep sending aid to Britain: our first line of defence and our only remaining friend.' Democrat F.D.R. likewise campaigned on 'All aid to the Allies short of war' – coupled with: 'Your boys are not going to be sent into any foreign wars.'

After the election, US Ambassador to London Joe Kennedy returned home for good and told the *Boston Globe*: 'Democracy is finished in England. It may be here … The whole reason for aiding England is to give us time … to prepare. It isn't that she's fighting for democracy. That's the bunk. She's fighting for self-preservation.' Roosevelt, though he owed no loyalty – legally, ancestrally, politically or emotionally – to the Empire that America had fought against in 1776 in order to win its democracy, knew it was not as simple as that for very many Americans.

Currently lying secure in Fort Knox was a manuscript that the British Government had loaned for the 1939 World's Fair that was too precious to risk on the high seas back to Britain in 1940. In a world submitting to the triumph of brute force, it spoke in a silent, yet perhaps stronger, voice than any living politician the promise of the rule of law that still bound these two very different democracies together. The translation from the Latin of clauses 39 and 40 of the Magna Carta were the crux of it.

'No free man shall be seized, imprisoned, dispossessed, outlawed, exiled or deprived of his standing in any way, nor will we act with force against him, or send others to do so, except by the lawful judgment of his peers and according to the law of the land', said one. The other: 'To no one will we sell, to no one will we deny or delay, right or justice.' It was a bit long-winded, and you would need to explain almost 750 years of history to relate how that promise had wound up in the America of 1940. But it was one of the reasons E.B. White, encountering Nazi admirers and appeasers in New York, knew that he believed that being an

American meant: 'a human being should live free'. Many wars had been sold as the battle between good and evil – might it actually be true of this one? There was a saying that all that was necessary for evil to triumph was that good men do nothing, and US journalist Eric Sevareid had witnessed this doing nothing for himself over Christmas 1938, visiting a charming, fairytale village in Bavaria. Four years before, it had welcomed Hitler to witness the 300th anniversary of its famous Passion Play. Eric had been charmed by its houses painted with Bible scenes and messages of brotherly love; chilled that every door was decked with wreath and holly – and an ugly black and red placard declaring *Juden Unerwünscht*. The ubiquitous message even appeared by the cash register in the home of a famous former Christ. 'You see, we have nothing to say about it,' explained the sweet-looking cashier. 'They just come and put it up and we have nothing to say about it.' Surely, Eric suggested, it wasn't necessary here in Oberammergau? Were there even any Jews? He hadn't seen any. 'There was one,' she replied, 'He was a Catholic, too. They took him away.'

ABOVE: With Chartwell largely mothballed 'for the duration', the Prime Minister's official residence at Chequers saw high-level discussions between Churchill and scientists working nearby.

Ironically, under Prime Minister Churchill, you could now be imprisoned without trial in Britain too, thanks to the infamous '18B' clause of the 1939 Defence Regulations relating to persons of 'hostile origin or associations'. When, in 1936, Churchill's actress daughter Sarah had fled to New York to marry Austrian-born entertainer Vic Oliver (hotly pursued by brother Randolph and the British press), one major element in her father's disapproval, he told her, was that in any coming war her husband's nationality could see her designated an 'enemy'. Churchill personally hated 18B and thought it ran counter to British values. But faced, in the aftermath of Dunkirk, with what to do with avowed fascists and 'enemy aliens' (citizens of hostile nations) whose classification had not yet been processed, he had thought it wisest to bite the bullet and 'collar the lot'.

The U-boat sinking of the *Arandora Star*, with a mixture of enemy aliens and prisoners of war aboard, in July 1940, ended the transportation of internees to Canada. And non-hostile 'enemy aliens' were progressively released through 1940 or 1941. Most were in Britain precisely because they were anti-Nazi, and H.G. Wells had been one of those who made 'a considerable row about the

ABOVE: Churchill in Bristol, April 1941. Goebbels envied the propaganda value of his readiness to walk among the people after raids – he could never persuade Hitler to do it.

persecution of refugees,' George Orwell noted. Wells had attributed this more to the War Office than to Winston, who was, he told Orwell, 'a good man'.

Clementine Churchill was unresponsive to the complaints of her cousin (and bridesmaid) Sydney Mitford about the imprisonment under 18B of Sydney's Fascist daughter Diana Mosley in Holloway. Clementine said the Mosleys were safer in prison than on the streets, where they might be lynched. Winston, after considerable lobbying, let Oswald join his wife in a special wing in Holloway.

The Government wanted to be fair to everyone, 'including Fascists – they're human beings,' Labour Home Secretary Herbert Morrison explained to the *Daily Express* in December 1940, but this was wartime. 'In peacetime the British would never stand for it – at least, I hope they wouldn't!' Labour remained strongly against releasing Fascists and, later in the war, it was Clementine who advised Winston against pushing to abolish 18B as it might split his Government. In the end, it was Morrison who released the Mosleys to house arrest on health grounds.

Back in November 1940, the British Ambassador to the US had returned after his discreet withdrawal during the Presidential election, with a message for the press. 'Well, boys, Britain's broke; it's your money we want,' Lord Lothian declared cheerily – and more than once – for the cameras. In his Fireside Chat on 29th December, Franklin Roosevelt declared that America would become 'the arsenal of democracy'. By the time it arrived at the House of Representatives in April 1941, the 'Lend-Lease' Bill (H.R. 1776 as chance ironically numbered it) gave shape to Roosevelt's folksy 'fire hose' imagery. American industry would gear up for military production and go to work producing what Britain needed to fight on; both sides could worry about the money later.

US warships also began to accompany vital food convoys to besieged Britain (which, Hitler was warned, postponed his promised U-boat victory in the Battle of the Atlantic). In August 1941, Churchill secretly sailed to Newfoundland for a face-to-face meeting with Roosevelt, where the two 'ex-naval persons' drafted and signed the Atlantic Charter, a brief statement of the freedoms Britain was fighting for and to which any future Allies could sign up.

'The Lease-Lend Bill must be regarded without question as the most unsordid act in the whole of recorded history,' Churchill told the City at the Mansion House in November 1941. But lend-leased arms had barely started to arrive before, on 7th December 1941, without warning, the Japanese Empire attacked the US Pacific fleet at Pearl Harbor in Hawaii, before sailing south to invade British, Dutch and American Pacific territories.

The world had changed overnight. Stalin, realising Japan no longer posed an immediate threat to him, immediately began to shift Siberian troops to the defence of Moscow against Germany. Roosevelt declared war on the Japanese; Churchill followed suit. That night he also sent a 'Most Immediate' telegram to neutral Eire.

Received, DUBLIN, 00.30 8 December 1941
Following from Prime Minister for Mr. de Valera. Personal, private and secret.
Begins. Now is your chance. Now or never. 'A Nation once again'. Am very ready to meet you at any time. Ends.

What precisely did that mean? De Valera never responded to find out.

For four excruciating days, what the bombing of Pearl Harbor was going to mean for Britain's war remained unclear. In America, the President's advisor J.K. Galbraith recorded his fear that popular fury against the Japanese might force a purely Pacific war, leaving Roosevelt 'unable from then on to give more than purely peripheral help to Britain.'

But then, four days after Pearl Harbor, first Mussolini, then Hitler, declared war on the United States in support of their Axis partner Japan – and Roosevelt declared war on Germany later the same day. 'It was truly astounding,' said Galbraith of Hitler's decision. 'I cannot tell you our feelings of triumph. It was a totally irrational thing for him to do, and I think it saved Europe.' Winston Churchill, when writing his history of the war, had no doubt: 'No American will think it wrong of me if I proclaim that to have the United States at our side was to me the greatest joy.' His overwhelming feeling was:

So we had won after all! Yes, after Dunkirk; after the fall of France; after the horrible episode of Oran; after the threat of invasion ... after the deadly struggle of the U-boat – the Battle of the Atlantic, gained by a hand's breadth ... we had won the war. England would live; Britain would live; the Commonwealth of Nations and the Empire would live ... Being saturated and satiated with emotion and sensation, I went to bed and slept the sleep of the saved and thankful.

OPPOSITE: Firemen 'dig for victory' in the shadow of St Paul's. The Blitz was over but not the struggle for survival, as the Battle of the Atlantic raged to keep Britain fed and supplied with arms.

PART FIVE

1942–65

CHAPTER 14

'This is a very hard war'

Of course the war was not won in December 1941. It would be another year before Churchill could even venture that the Allies were, perhaps, looking at 'the end of the beginning'. But his personal war – the one only he could fight, only he could win, the one for which he alone was the indispensable man – was done. He had spent a year and a half hanging on by his fingertips; steadfastly directing his thoughts to the 'broad sunlit uplands' above, while all too aware of the 'abyss' below; every dawn a new day when it could all come crashing down. For, in truth, every day had been another Battle of Britain Day – the odds great, the margins small, the stakes infinite. Now at last Churchill could feel solid ground beneath his feet; could now begin the climb.

But in what might be seen as an anxious dawn awakening after the 'sleep of the saved and thankful', Churchill realised that, without America's agreement to focus on beating Hitler *before* they took on Japan together, nothing had changed. Just getting President Roosevelt to take his meeting (codenamed Arcadia) over Christmas and New Year was a victory.

OPPOSITE: Mary Churchill (in the ATS) shows how a fighter takes on a V-1 rocket during the 1944 'Second Blitz'. Diana was an air raid warden, while Sarah, in the WAAF, often acted as her father's aide-de-camp.

Once in Washington, Churchill argued – against Roosevelt's advice from his own Chiefs of Staff – for 'Europe First': the Pacific War would not be abandoned, but the European War was to take priority. Alongside Winston sat British Chiefs of Staff who had been fighting Hitler for 18 months; Roosevelt's Chiefs were untried in modern warfare and in the Pacific had just suffered a devastating loss. It would take time to establish a working relationship, and it was clear that Roosevelt had no interest in maintaining the British Empire. But the American President became adamant for 'Europe First'; it was a start.

While staying at the White House, Churchill suffered a mild heart attack; his personal doctor Charles Wilson (later Lord Moran) decided to tell no one, not even Churchill himself, simply advising him to take things easy for a while. Churchill made a trip to Ottawa, where he made a speech to the Canadian Parliament. 'When the invasion season returns,' he warned, Canadian troops might be involved in 'one of the most frightful battles the world has ever seen'. But he revisited his 1940 experience of trying to get the French to fight on from their North African colonies; when he had said Britain would fight on, the French generals had said: 'In three weeks England will have her neck wrung like a chicken.' Churchill paused for the applause and stamping to die down. 'Some chicken,' he said. More stamping, applause, and laughter. 'Some neck.' The whole of Parliament rose to its feet.

ABOVE: Churchill in the Map Room of his underground bunker in Whitehall. He had become Prime Minister at a time when Britain's survival was one piece in an intricate global jigsaw puzzle of warfare and politics.

Churchill's plan now was an Anglo-American capture of those Vichy France colonies of Morocco and Algeria in 'Operation Torch'. The British were already engaged in Egypt; once won, North Africa would become a 'springboard not a sofa': a land base for the invasion of Europe from the Mediterranean, its 'soft underbelly'.

The heads of the US Army and Navy refused to approve 'Torch', preferring their own 'Operation Sledgehammer' – invading France's Channel coast in the summer of 1942. The British thought this would be suicidal. A furious Roosevelt called General Marshall and Admiral King into the White House and issued a direct order to approve 'Torch': one of only two direct orders of the war. They put command of 'Torch' under the relatively lowly two-star Major General Dwight D. Eisenhower.

••• ——————— •••

In Buckingham Palace, the King's private secretary Tommy Lascelles' view of Noel Coward's new film *In Which We Serve* on 23th October 1942 was somewhat impeded by the Prime Minister, like 'a cat on hot bricks', waiting for news from Number 10 on the launch of a critical battle in Egypt. When Tommy left and returned quietly with the message that the news was good, Churchill insisted on hearing for himself, astonishing the footmen along the route back from his phone call with a rendition of 'Roll Out The Barrel' delivered, 'with gusto, but with little evidence of musical talent.'

The film screening was for the Mountbattens and guest of honour Eleanor Roosevelt and her son Elliott. Eleanor was in Britain on a fact-finding mission for her husband, including meeting some of the many American GIs now stationed there. 'Dearest Franklin,' she wrote from Chequers on 25th October, 'The Prime Minister is pleased with the ham & honey … Saw a lot of boys at the Red + … they came in with terrible blisters because their socks are too tight. All coming here should be issued wool socks. No heat is allowed till Nov. & most of them have colds … The spirit of the English people is something to bow down to …'

Clementine and Eleanor would broadcast together later in the war; one of Clemmie's many alliances with the wives of men useful to her husband, from US newsman Ed Murrow's wife Janet to the Soviet Ambassador's wife Agniya Maisky. Her husband Ivan had been impressed with Clemmie – a 'lively intelligent woman who was interested in politics and understood it' – on their first meeting at Chartwell in the 1930s. 'I tell her everything,' Winston told him then, 'But she knows how to keep mum.' In wartime, one Washington newspaper called Clementine 'Winston's greatest asset'.

'Operation Torch' was launched in November 1942. The Anglo-American forces came as liberators not invaders, which meant Eisenhower, operating from Gibraltar, had not only to liaise with the British but to negotiate the triangular politics of the Pétain administration in Vichy, the local commanders in its colonies and his Free French ally General de Gaulle: just a taste of the complexities to come. As the Allies powered to a swift victory in North Africa, Hitler occupied the whole of the rest of France. The following day, the battle in Egypt whose beginning had set Winston singing down the corridors of Buckingham Palace came to an end in victory at El Alamein: the victory he hailed as perhaps 'the end of the beginning.'

In New York that Christmas, the premiere of a film based on an unperformed play called *Everybody Comes to Rick's* (picked up by Warner Brothers just after Pearl Harbor) was rushed forward to make the most of Americans' jubilation at their North African success. If you've ever struggled with the complex international

ABOVE: Eleanor Roosevelt and Clementine Churchill worked well together – here addressing the Canadian people together over the radio in 1944.

politics behind the romance in *Casablanca*, spare a thought for Eisenhower. Spare a thought for Winston Churchill.

Because, of course, this wasn't even half the war the Allies were fighting. On 19th November, General Zhukov halted the German advance into the Soviet Union. The Battle of Stalingrad, perhaps the single largest battle in human history, had been raging since August and, by the beginning of February 1943, Hitler had lost 800,000 men – killed, injured or captured. Soviet troops recovered a quarter of a million corpses from the ruins, while their own dead, injured and captured numbered over a million, plus 40,000 civilian deaths.

Stalingrad truly was 'one of the most frightful battles the world has ever seen'; a city whose vast mass, 'fought street by street', had devoured an entire hostile army. Just as Churchill had envisaged London might have to do – before it was saved by 22 miles of choppy sea and a multinational force of young men in aeroplanes. 'Never in the field of human conflict ...' Now all Britain celebrated the victory of 'Uncle Joe' Stalin as if it was their own.

Churchill had always known it might come to this: Britain fighting alongside the Soviets. Ivan Maisky had been dumbstruck on that first visit to Chartwell during the 1938 Sudeten Crisis, when Winston produced pre-Revolutionary vodka and told him that there was a 1793 bottle of wine in his cellar for a 'very special, truly exceptional occasion', promising they'd drink it together when Britain and Russia beat Hitler. 'Churchill's hatred of Berlin really has gone beyond all limits!' Maisky recorded.

Shortly afterwards, the Nazi-Soviet non-aggression pact had scuppered Neville Chamberlain's hopes of preventing Hitler's march into Poland, then Hitler and Stalin had carved Poland up between them.

Maisky had found it 'very strange and nonsensical' of Churchill, early in his premiership, to tell him he was unconcerned with Anglo-Soviet relations at present, as war between the Nazis and the USSR was inevitable and Stalin would approach England as soon as the German guns started firing on its borders.

Once they did start firing, Churchill was not among those who thought Hitler would find the Soviet Union a feeble foe. 'I will bet you a Monkey to a Mousetrap [500-1],' he told doubters in April 1941, 'that the Russians are still fighting, and fighting victoriously, two years from now.' General Alan Brooke had been one of the doubters. Looking back on New Year's Day 1943 to how things had looked a year before, he wrote: 'I felt Russia could never hold ... and Abadan [oil refinery] would be captured with consequent collapse of Middle East, India etc. England would again be bombarded, threat of invasion revived ...'

Brooke was Chief of the Imperial General Staff, one of the military men with whom Churchill restrained his 'natural pugnacity' by sitting on his own head. Or sometimes not: 'When I thump the table and push my face towards him what does he do?' he said of Brooke: 'Thumps the table harder and glares back at me.' Churchill had appointed Brooke in December 1941, and they saw out the war together. Winston the young Gentleman Cadet at Sandhurst would have be amazed – and surely more than a little delighted – to know that, in aftertimes, the rights and wrongs of the passionate debates between Winston Churchill and his generals,

'I will unsay no word I have spoken about it. But all this fades away before the spectacle which is unfolding.'

his admirals, his air marshals and his allies would become as lively a topic of debate for future cadets as the Battle of Thermopylae – and perhaps as long to be argued over.

When Churchill announced back in June 1941 that the Soviet Union had joined the Allies, he was frank with the British people about his seeming volte-face after a quarter of a century of anti-Bolshevism: 'I will unsay no word I have spoken about it. But all this fades away before the spectacle which is unfolding.'

The BBC had then faced the problem of whether to play the 'Internationale' (which, Maisky said, made the 'hair of a thousand British Blimps' stand on end) alongside all the other Allied anthems on Sundays. The anthem of international Communism on the BBC was where Churchill drew the line, Maisky was told. Tuning in with interest that first Sunday, he heard instead, a Russian folk tune. 'Very beautiful' – but probably more recognisable to Britons than Russians by the end of six months, at which point 'Internationale' was cleared for use on the BBC. ('We are asked not to overdo it.')

Fighting a world war as an unlikely triumvirate with Roosevelt and Stalin might not have been Churchill's ideal scenario – his first choice would have been resolving Germany's Danzig grievance in 1932 and having some chance of there being no war at all. But as his Soviet ally's founding philosopher had said: 'Men make their own history, but they do not make it as they please.' So Churchill gave Stalin whatever support he could, as soon as he could.

Arctic convoys began in August 1941 and, by the end of that year, 99 out of the 100 merchant ships had arrived safely with their vital supplies, thanks to the Royal Navy and the information coming through Enigma. Merchant seamen and

OPPOSITE: Fortune makes strange bedfellows, and Churchill had no qualms about supporting the Soviet war effort against Hitler. Stalin's later actions in Eastern Europe appalled him.

sailors continued to brave these terrible conditions throughout the war. As with the all-important Battle of the Atlantic, Bletchley Park's Enigma information on the whereabouts of German U-boats was key. But whenever the Germans changed their codes, casualties soared until the information flow began again. Churchill also fed Stalin vital, precise Enigma information about German battle plans, without revealing its source.

Of course what Stalin really wanted from Churchill was an invasion of France as soon as possible, as a Second Front to divide Hitler's armies in two. Britain, fighting alone, could not give him that in the summer of 1941. Nor in 1942, though Enigma intercepts showed Hitler had diverted planes from the Russian Front to fight the Allies in North Africa. Throughout the war, Churchill's determination was always to harry the enemy in every way possible, from the sabotage by the Special Operations Executive to ever-heavier bombing raids on Germany, which weakened the German war effort for Russia's sake as much as Britain's.

'Bomber' Harris had stood on the Air Ministry roof on the night of 29th December 1940 watching the City of London burn. Tens of thousands of small incendiary bombs had started so many fires that in some areas it created a firestorm, devouring Wren church, workshop and warehouse alike. 'Well,' he said to Air Marshal Portal, who he had brought up to see what was happening, 'They have

sown the wind …' Churchill, too, had referenced Hosea in his Ottawa speech, 'Hitler and his Nazi gang have sown the wind, let them reap the whirlwind.'

'This is a very hard war,' Churchill told members of his party in 1942.

> Its numerous and fearful problems reach down to the very foundations of human society. Its scope is worldwide, and it involves all nations and every man, woman, and child in them. Strategy and economics are interwoven. Sea, land, and air are but a single service. The latest refinements of science are linked with the cruelties of the Stone Age.

When the atom had been split a decade earlier by two Cambridge scientists, one dismissed as 'moonshine' talk of unlimited nuclear power; but a Hungarian refugee who read the news was crossing the road in London when he suddenly realised the potential of a chain reaction to release explosive power of unimaginable magnitude. In 1940, two more refugee scientists in Birmingham worked out on

ABOVE: Eisenhower (centre) would combine the efforts of the British and American services in 'Overlord', the invasion of Western Europe in 1944, while Stalin fought on against Hitler in the East.

the back of an envelope that, theoretically, a huge atomic bomb would require not the tons of uranium that had been thought, but a single kilogram.

In what he called the 'Wizard War' of destructive science, Churchill could not have stopped the coming of atomic bombs: the Americans, Germans and Soviets all had atomic programmes, though the British were by far the most advanced. But by sharing British research with the still-neutral but better resourced Americans through the transatlantic Tizard Mission, he accelerated the speed of development to the point where it could play a role in this war – and on the Allied side. Later in the war, the coming of Britain's 'Second Blitz' by V-1 and V-2 rocket hinted how suddenly the Wizard War could switch sides.

Alongside its technology of death, Britain had shared a secret with neutral America in 1941 that has saved an estimated 200 million lives so far – penicillin. The pioneering work of Australian Howard Florey and German-Jewish refugee Ernst Chain at Oxford University, inspired by an old scientific paper by Alexander Fleming, was now given American production capacity, and the first successful treatment for the septicaemia that had robbed Winston Churchill of both his mother and daughter came in 1942: of a young American woman who went on to live for another 50 years. It would be in mass production in time for the invasion of Europe.

Breakthrough technologies could come from anywhere, in any field, and Churchill relied heavily on the wide-ranging advice of 'the Prof', who he had appointed as his Chief Scientific Adviser – with mixed results. The clear, graphic mapping of many aspects of the war, at home and abroad, that Lindemann's statistics branch could provide was essential to Churchill's decision-making. Sometimes, though, when those decisions proved to be wrong – and in some cases the cost in human lives was very great – the questionable reassurance the statistics played their part. But while he had his critics within the high echelons of those directing the war, Lindemann: 'hated Hitler and all his works and his contribution to Hitler's downfall in all sorts of odd ways was considerable,' in the judgement of Churchill's Chief Staff Officer, General Hastings 'Pug' Ismay.

While some might have questioned Churchill's reliance on 'the Prof', none queried the Chief Staff Officer he chose in April 1940, while still at the Admiralty. Ismay and his small team quietly acted as the flexible joint between Government and military to give Churchill control – though not too much – of the minutiae of managing a war. Perhaps no one knew better how to handle Winston for his own good – except Clemmie of course. Ismay concluded that without his wife, the 'history of Winston Churchill and of the world would have been a very different story'.

BRITISH WARSHIPS
KEEP OPEN 80,000 MILES OF
SEA ROUTES

Never less than 600 British warships and nearly 2,000 merchant ships are at sea from **BRITISH PORTS** at any given time . . . . . .

Her first role was still to support Winston, taking infinite pains to protect the emotional and physical well-being of her husband. But she would not hesitate to intervene more directly. As early as June 1940 she was minuting his principal private secretary, demanding to know what was being done about shelters for the bombed and compensation for the injured; welfare payments and morale-boosting activities. As the public began addressing their plaints to her mailbag, she came to be seen as the caring face of her husband's premiership.

Amidst war, Churchill's coalition also gave thought to peace – to 'Where will we go when we win?' Attlee's Labour deputy Greenwood pushed for reform of the whole area of social insurance and allied services and in November 1942 an inter-departmental committee chaired by Liberal economist William Beveridge, who had worked on Winston's reforms at the Board of Trade, 30 years before, produced a report that became the basis of the post-war Welfare State.

Churchill and Beveridge were both great believers in social insurance, on the German model that inspired them back in 1908. In summer 1940, Churchill's war damage insurance scheme, paid for by a new property tax, was designed to share the burden of war losses, 'evenly on the shoulders of the nation'.

Now Beveridge suggested the same for tackling the five 'giant evils' of Want, Disease, Ignorance, Squalor and Idleness. A new National Health Service, funded by a similar insurance scheme, was envisaged in a 1944 report produced by Health Minister Henry Willink. However, though it supplied its impetus, the post-war NHS was not ultimately shaped by Churchill's wartime government but by his most formidable adversary in the Commons throughout the War. Aneurin Bevan would set up Britain's NHS funded from general taxation rather than the 'insurance stamps' of Willink's scheme, ensuring even the most expensive treatment would be free for even the poorest patient, based purely on the basis of clinical need. 'If you hadn't fully paid up,' said Bevan, 'You couldn't have a second-class operation, could you?' Bevan's oft-repeated phrase 'This is my truth, tell me yours' shows a Churchillian respect for the importance of democratic debate and, though sworn enemies, their battles royal in the Commons (one post-war cartoon pictured the two men as giants among Lilliputians) demonstrated the robustness of the institution for making peaceful progress.

And still the war rolled on. For Britain, it was the almost invisible war at sea, the Battle of the Atlantic, that came closest to defeating it. Not the clash of giant

OPPOSITE: The Royal and Allied navies backed up the merchant fleet delivering food and supplies all around the world in a huge and desperately complex operation.

155

dreadnoughts in set-piece battles, but the U-boats hunting down convoys that brought war materials and the food to make up what the British could never produce themselves: no matter how well they managed their rations, no matter how much they 'Dug for Victory'. Office boy Colin Perry, who had been in the City in the first week of the Blitz and found himself pictured on the front page of the newspaper alongside Winston Churchill, and thought the caption might be 'Present, Future', had ambitions to become a fighter pilot. But lacking the necessary School Certificate, he had settled for the Merchant Navy – once a friend reassured him it was even more dangerous, since pilots were only a target while in the air. And indeed, one in four merchant seamen (though not Colin himself) lost their lives in the course of this war.

As Britain's population swelled by a million with American and Canadian troops readying for the invasion of Europe in the summer of 1944, vastly increasing her need for supplies, her war in the Far East was going badly. The fall of Singapore in February 1942 had been one of Churchill's worst military defeats, and Japan had gone on to occupy Burma, driving half a million refugees into neighbouring Bengal. This was to be just one more factor in an unfolding tragedy of famine and disease that killed perhaps two million people in Bengal, dwarfing all other Indian, British, Anzac, Canadian and American war deaths combined. Besides the natural disasters of poor harvest and cyclone that peacetime Bengal could probably have coped with, wartime conditions by land and sea, and many military and political decisions, at provincial, national, and imperial level, right up to the British cabinet and Churchill himself, contributed to a disaster that no one had sought and served no one.

••• ———— •••

Through these years, Churchill threw himself around the world by air and sea with an alacrity that was the despair of those who would rather he stayed alive a while longer. But since his meeting with Roosevelt that had produced the Atlantic Charter in August 1941, he was convinced that face-to-face conferences by those at the top could achieve a unity of purpose as nothing else could. He attended a further 15 over the next four years, only one of them – the Commonwealth Leaders' Conference – in London.

The first of the 'Big Three' conferences was held in Tehran in November 1943. Stalin finally got his Second Front: Roosevelt and Churchill agreed that summer of 1944 would see them ready for the invasion of France. Churchill's expectation of a swift collapse of Italy and invasion of southern Europe had been disappointed when

Hitler took over Italy's defence, and preparations for D-Day now took priority for resources and men.

Churchill, who had been giving thought to how an army could invade by sea ever since Dunkirk, suggested the basic idea that became the 'Mulberry Harbours', floating harbours that were sailed across the sea with the invaders. Admiral Ramsay, who Churchill had coaxed out of retirement when he was at the Admiralty in 1939, had overseen the rescue of the BEF with 700 ships in 1940. Now he would command the 7,000 taking the Allies back in 'Operation Neptune'. Eisenhower, now a four-star General, was in overall control of 'Operation Overlord'.

Churchill enthused the King, a veteran of the Battle of Jutland in the last war, with the idea that they could watch the D-Day landings together from the deck of HMS *Belfast*. Ramsay flatly refused to take either of them; Tommy Lascelles diplomatically asked the King what advice he would be giving his 18-year-old daughter Princess Elizabeth about choosing a new Prime Minister if the ship was sunk; after which a letter from the King to Churchill put paid to the idea. (Not that Churchill could be kept away from the invasion forces for long.)

Now all the Allies were engaged in the same continent came the question of what kind of continent it would become. The Western Front and Eastern Front were now advancing towards each other on Germany, and at Yalta the 'Big Three' made a 'Declaration on Liberated Europe', pledging to help the forming of interim governments: 'broadly representative of all democratic elements in the population and pledged to the earliest possible establishment, through free elections, of governments responsive to the will of the people.' However the fate of the Warsaw Uprising in the autumn of 1944, when the Red Army had held back and let Nazis

ABOVE: The summits between Stalin, Roosevelt and Churchill (here with daughter Sarah and Anthony Eden in Tehran) were vital, but Churchill believed Roosevelt gave too much ground to Stalin at Yalta.

crush the uprising, had Churchill progressively more worried about the fate of Eastern and Central Europe – Poland and Greece in particular.

A week after D-Day, the first V-1 rocket fell on London. People were more shaken, in many ways, by this than the first Blitz. The sudden cut-out of the engine of a 'doodlebug' or the silent arrival of the 'flying gas pipe' (the first V2s had been reported as gas explosions) were especially demoralising after the uplift of D-Day. When, in August 1944, Roosevelt's Treasury Secretary asked to tour London's air raid shelters, it was Clementine who escorted him, as the figure of Government authority less likely to provoke public anger. She and Winston worried about Diana, 'in the thick of it' as an air raid warden, according to her sister Mary (who was herself in an ack-ack battery in the middle of Hyde Park). Sarah was in the WAAF and often travelled with her father, but their brother Randolph, who had joined the army on the outbreak of war, had been largely kept away from active service overseas – his famous surname made him too rich a prize.

ABOVE: Churchill crossing the Rhine in March 1945 with Montgomery, Alan Brooke and US General Simpson.
OPPOSITE: Churchill flew thousands of miles – for high-level negotiations or as a vital morale-booster for ordinary troops. Here they gather in the old Roman amphitheatre at Carthage, Tunisia to hear him.

On 12th April 1945, two months after Yalta, the US President died and Churchill paid tribute: 'In Franklin Roosevelt there died the greatest American friend we have ever known.' On 30th April, Adolf Hitler killed himself in his bunker and a succession of surrenders of German forces in different countries began.

On 4th May, in a top-secret cable, Churchill told Anthony Eden to expect another 'Big Three' Conference in July with Stalin and Roosevelt's successor Harry Truman 'in some unshattered town in Germany, if such can be found,' and warned they might be facing 'an event in the history of Europe to which there has been no parallel … the vast zone of Russian-controlled Europe, not necessarily economically Sovietised but police-governed'.

> We have several powerful bargaining counters on our side, the use of which might make for a peaceful agreement … If they are not settled before the United States Armies withdraw from Europe and the Western world folds up its war machines, there are no prospects of a satisfactory solution and very little of preventing a third World War.

Winston's wife was at that moment in Russia. As head of the Red Cross Fund raising money for relief work there, Clementine had been invited to meet Stalin at the Kremlin. Winston was anxious that between touring hospitals and posing for photographs she should send any information gleaned from Stalin, or from the leader of Yugoslavia's Communist partisans, Josip Tito, whom she invited to a vodka-fuelled afternoon tea. On 7th May, Clementine Churchill was awarded the Order of the Red Banner of Labour and thanked for the tremendous work she had done for the Red Army. The following day, 8th May 1945, hostilities in Europe officially ceased. She could not write to Winston, only send a cable, but perhaps it said it all.

'ALL MY THOUGHTS ARE WITH YOU ON THIS SUPREME DAY MY DARLING STOP IT COULD NOT HAVE HAPPENED WITHOUT YOU.'

Churchill, out on a balcony of the Ministry of Health with Ernie Bevin, waving to thousands of people who felt the same, said, 'This is your victory. Victory of the cause of freedom in every land. In all our long history, we have never seen a greater day than this.'

The war could now switch wholeheartedly to the defeat of Japan, but Britain was safe, and something like normal life could start to resume. Attlee went to Blackpool in May for the Labour Party Conference and, just as a phone call from Bournemouth had begun this great adventure together, so a call from Blackpool ended it: the Labour Party had voted to withdraw from the National Government, there would need to be an election.

It would be the first in ten years; the first since the one in 1935 that was won by Baldwin – a lifetime ago. This would be the first chance anyone under 30 had to have a say in shaping the future they had been fighting for. Churchill bid farewell to his Labour colleagues with tears in his eyes.

But when he contemplated socialists in government, commanding the immense powers he had commanded for the last five years, he feared the worst. On 4th June he broadcast a speech – against Clementine's better advice – saying that no socialist government could risk free speech and 'would have to fall back on some form of Gestapo'. It only confirmed for many voters that a great war leader was not their man to build the peace.

On 17th July, Attlee accompanied Churchill to the Potsdam Conference of the 'Big Three' in occupied Germany. Churchill was relieved to find that Harry Truman seemed like a man he could do business with. He and Attlee took a break back in London for the election results – which had been held up until 26th July to allow the troops' votes to be counted.

Stalin was astonished to learn that a landslide victory had delivered Labour three million more votes and 200 more seats than Churchill's party, and that Attlee would be returning to the conference at Potsdam as Prime Minister. So too were some voters: when 12-year-old Czech *Kindertransport* refugee Alf Dubs, holidaying near Blackpool, brought back to his boarding house the 'lunchtime score' of 120 seats to 30 so far, someone said, 'Oh my God, it's the end of England!'

The apocryphal quote 'The country will never stand for it!' is ascribed to variously a senior naval officer, a lady in a grand hotel and an ousted minister.

But Winston Churchill's words were recorded by Captain Pim, who brought the news to the Prime Minister in his bath. Churchill turned grey and Pim thought he would faint. Then he delivered what may perhaps be Winston Churchill's greatest speech of the war: 'They are perfectly entitled to vote as they please. This is democracy. This is what we've been fighting for.'

ABOVE: No greater day – Churchill stands overlooking the crowds in Whitehall the day that Victory in Europe was declared.

CHAPTER 15

'An iron curtain'

After a farewell Cabinet, Churchill told Anthony Eden – who would become his Deputy Opposition Leader – that 30 years of his life had been passed in this room, but he would never sit here again. The British political system is ruthless – Prime Ministers must vacate Downing Street the day they lose office. In 1940, Winston had been gracious to the ailing Chamberlain, letting him and Mrs Chamberlain stay in the upper floors of No. 10 while he lived in Admiralty House; now Attlee granted the Churchills Chequers for one final weekend. At its end, after friends and family had signed the visitors' book, Churchill himself signed, then wrote '*Finis*'.

Clementine voiced the idea that being cast out of office might be a blessing in disguise, but at the end of August wrote a despairing letter to Mary: 'In our misery we seem, instead of clinging to each other to be always having scenes. I'm sure it is all my fault, but I'm finding life more than I can bear. He is so unhappy & that makes him very difficult ... I can't see any future.'

They were better off apart. Clemmie spent the autumn getting Chartwell, which had been mostly shut up during the war, ready for habitation, while Churchill set off for Lake Como in Italy, accompanied by daughter Sarah, his doctor, secretary, detective and valet. In a Europe still not without its dangers, he was provided with two aides-de-camp and 24 men from his own old 4th Hussars.

He wrote to Clemmie that he was painting again, 'much better in myself', with a growing relief that others would have to face 'the hideous problems of the aftermath'. Attlee's Government saw the ending of war with Japan on 15th August 1945 after two atomic explosions; the decision to pursue an independent nuclear deterrent; Indian independence and Partition; the expiry of the Mandate in Palestine and Jordan; the Berlin Airlift; the start of the Malayan Emergency and (after another, much narrower, election victory in 1950) the Korean War. All this in a time of severe financial reckoning ... 'Hideous' does not sound too strong.

OPPOSITE: The Churchills – and Rufus the dog – take tea at Chartwell in 1947. With the youthful politician, quite literally, behind her, Clemmie might have hoped politics would be also. But Winston's retirement would have to wait.

Churchill's return to England in October 1945 saw him cut off from the stream of top-level information on the international situation, and facing the unrewarding task of acting as Leader of the Opposition to a landslide government. Politics, 'still his mistress, had rebuffed and rejected him,' said his daughter Sarah, 'Publicly and witheringly in the face of the world, but he was still her servant and would withdraw to the perimeter of her affection, ensconce himself firmly at her door and without her even noticing it begin to play once more the role of an ardent suitor and sometimes a cheeky one.'

His interventions in the House were certainly lively, but his attendance erratic. Though he usually presided over meetings of the Shadow Cabinet, he would sometimes insist on holding them over lunch at the Savoy hotel. Anthony Eden manned the fort on Winston's lengthy absences abroad. These trips were not, however, all mere holiday – and Westminster was not Churchill's only stage.

In February 1946, he arrived in New York to public honours and a ticker-tape parade. He spent six weeks sunbathing and swimming – most of them in Florida, but one in Cuba, scene of his first foreign adventure. He and Clemmie arrived at

Rancho Boyeros on an aircraft provided by President Truman, to the welcome of a large crowd and a limousine sent by President Ramón Grau San Martín, with whom he waved to crowds from the balcony. Ernest Hemingway invited him on a fishing trip. Cigar manufacturers sent box after box to his suite.

From there, at the invitation of President Truman, he went to speak at Westminster College in Fulton, Missouri on 5th March 1946. It was not a short speech – almost 5,000 words – but as so often, one or two phrases would resonate: one was the idea of a 'special relationship' between the British Commonwealth and Empire and the United States. The other: 'From Stettin in the Baltic to Trieste in the Adriatic, an iron curtain has descended across the Continent …'

Churchill said he did not think Soviet Russia wanted war, but he feared their desire for 'an indefinite expansion of their power and doctrines.' What he suggested now as a counterbalance – a way to avoid a 'quivering, precarious balance of power' – was an international alliance. 'If the population of the English-speaking Commonwealth be added to that of the United States with all that such co-operation implies … ' there would be 'no temptation to ambition or adventure. On the contrary, there will be an overwhelming assurance of security.'

This should, he suggested, be done within the framework of the United Nations – the body that had grown out of the 1942 Declaration of the United States, Britain and other Allies into a Charter and world organisation. Theirs would be a friendship into which a peaceable Soviet Union would be welcomed.

The *Wall Street Journal* declared that it wanted no such alliance with any other nation. The *Chicago Sun* inveighed against the 'poisonous doctrines' of Fulton. In London, *The Times* mentioned the 'perhaps less happy' passages of Churchill's speech. And while Attlee declined either to endorse or to dissociate himself from it, 93 Labour MPs put down a motion of censure against Churchill. In Moscow, Stalin declared, 'Mr Churchill and his friends' were offering an ultimatum: 'recognize our supremacy over you, voluntarily, and all will be well – otherwise war is inevitable.'

Those who saw Winston as a war-monger, and read only soundbites, got what they expected. Others read the whole thing and made up their own mind.

On 19th September 1946 he delivered another speech, at Zurich University, on what he clearly saw as a related cause. He sought 'the re-creation of the European family'; its first step 'a partnership between France and Germany.' It was an inspired

OPPOSITE: Churchill took his paintbrushes with him on the 1946 American trip that would become world-famous for his Fulton speech. This is his impression from the balcony of the Miami Surf Club in Florida.

but – so close to the war – hugely controversial doctrine. De Gaulle declared 'all Frenchmen' were deeply suspicious of it. But in May 1948, a conference in The Hague that Churchill initiated met with the aim of promoting a United Europe.

He failed to win strong all-party British support for the idea but spoke powerfully in favour of some sort of European parliament. 'Closer political unity,' he said, 'involves some sacrifice or merger of national sovereignty.' But might it not be possible instead, to regard it as a gradual assumption of a larger sovereignty which could actually protect each nation's 'diverse and distinctive customs and characteristics'? The following year a Council of Europe assembly was set up in Strasbourg, where Churchill addressed an open-air crowd 20,000-strong. The second year it met, the Germans were participants, as Churchill said they should have been from the start.

Britain was, he said at a European Movement rally on 28th November 1949, 'an integral part of Europe … But Britain cannot be thought of as a single state in

ABOVE: In Brussels at the 1949 European International Congress. Churchill's post-war motto was expressed as: 'In War: Resolution; In Defeat: Defiance; In Victory: Magnanimity; In Peace: Good Will.'
OPPOSITE: 'Member for Britain.' Robert Stewart Sherriffs' caricature in the *Sketch* showed his status as a world statesman and hero to match Marlborough – but could he ever again become Prime Minister?

isolation … We shall never do anything to weaken the ties of blood and sentiment and tradition and common interest which unite us with the other members of the British family of nations.' In the same year, speaking at the Massachusetts Institute of Technology, he made a speech of hope addressed to the people behind his 'iron curtain':

> Laws just or unjust may govern men's actions. Tyrannies may restrain and regulate their words. The machinery of propaganda may pack their minds with falsehoods and deny them truth for many generations of time. But the soul of man thus held in trance, or frozen in a long night, can be awakened by a spark coming from God knows where, and in a moment the whole structure of lies and oppression is on trial for its life. Peoples in bondage need never despair.

Back in Britain, his family was in transition, adjusting to the post-war world. In George VI's Birthday Honours of 1946, Clementine had been made a Dame of the British Empire in recognition of her war work, though she would never use the title. The following year Winston's much-loved brother Jack died. To Winston and Clemmie, their children were often a cause of anxiety. Winston had set out on fatherhood with no role model of how to do it – believing that giving his kittens the affection and indulgence that he had so yearned for himself would see all things come right. Perhaps every son wants to emulate their father – but what do you do if your father is Winston Churchill? You go into politics, you tell people your ideas are better than theirs, you sometimes lose your temper,

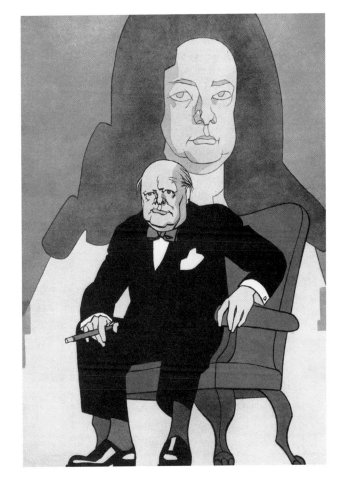

you drink with alacrity. But then you find it somehow doesn't work for you as it worked for him. Churchill felt 'a deep animal love' for Randolph; but every meeting between them ended in a 'bloody row'.

In the first days of the war Randolph, like so many young soldiers going off to fight, had made a hasty marriage but, like many such marriages, it had not survived the war. 'My mother was actually the fifth young lady to whom my father had proposed marriage in the three or four weeks since war had broken out,' said their son, another Winston, born at Chequers in 1940, 'and my mother was the first one to accept.' Debutante Pamela Digby was now Pamela Churchill but soon her relationship with Roosevelt's special envoy Averell Harriman was causing talk. 'It was,' said her son frankly, 'a rip-roaring wartime affair.' The couple divorced in 1946 and Randolph married again but this relationship too was in trouble.

Actress Sarah's marriage to Vic Oliver had also ended with the war and her parents were shocked when she married again in 1949 to photographer Antony Beauchamp, whom they had never even met. Diana too was experiencing difficulties in her marriage – her second – to the budding Conservative politician Duncan Sandys. Winston and Clemmie may have been taken aback by the whirlwind romance and 1947 wedding of their youngest, and happiest, daughter Mary to the young diplomat and politician Christopher Soames – but this marriage would last for 40 years until his death.

Chartwell was still Winston's much-loved haven – but no longer a worry. At the end of the war, hearing that Churchill might have to consider selling the estate, newspaper magnate Lord Camrose recruited a number of businessmen to purchase it and endow it as a trust, so that Winston and Clementine could enjoy it without anxiety for the rest of their lives. After that, it would pass to the National Trust as a permanent memorial to Britain's great war leader. Winston was delighted both with the idea of living there and that it would live on.

Once Churchill started writing again things had got much easier. Alexander Korda paid him an extraordinary £50,000 for the film rights to *A History of the English-Speaking Peoples*, whose first volume had been published in 1937. When another company paid £25,000 for copyright of his pre-war books he was able to purchase several farms adjacent to Chartwell. The flow of business, moreover, made him feel in the swim of things once again: teams of advisers and secretaries

OPPOSITE: As Prime Minister Attlee welcomes Queen Elizabeth to the 1951 Festival of Britain, billed as 'A Tonic for the Nation', Churchill bows to his wartime friend the King.

were recruited as he began work on his history of the war (though he once said, 'This is not history, this is my case.').

The Second World War kept him going through these years in Opposition – in more senses than one. The book would eventually run to nearly one and a half million words. He was able, in his uniquely privileged position, to obtain permission to reprint a stream of official wartime papers and *Life* magazine, amazingly, offered more than a million pounds (in 1940s money!) for first US serial rights.

The 1950 general election saw Labour win again; but with a much reduced majority, so Churchill was not downcast. (Not sufficiently downcast, certainly, to renounce the party leadership, as many – his wife included – would have wished.) When Attlee called another election in 1951 hoping for a stronger majority, the British electoral system played one of its wonted tricks. Labour got slightly more votes than the Conservatives but 26 fewer seats. At almost 77 years old – only Gladstone and Palmerston had been older – Winston Churchill was Prime Minister once again.

LEFT: Local MP Winston Churchill with Princess Elizabeth at the opening of an International Youth Centre in Chigwell. In a few months he would be Prime Minister; in a few more she would be Queen.

CHAPTER 16

'Meeting jaw to jaw is better than war'

Winston Churchill was once asked which year of his life he would like to live over again: '1940 every time', he replied unhesitatingly. Then, he had entered 10 Downing Street with one single, monumental task; now the tasks were just as monumental, though less heroic for the history books. The world of 1951 was transformed utterly from the one that had been left in 1939, and Churchill was much more responsive to the changes needed than many gave him credit for. To skip over his final ministry as a four-year swansong hiatus between Attlee's founding of the Welfare State and Anthony Eden's Suez Crisis debacle is to underestimate Churchill's achievements in moulding the post-war world.

Churchill had never fussed about party labels if a solution made sense, and the 'post-war consensus' that would persist for a quarter of a century bears his stamp. Labour's post-war settlement – from rail nationalisation to Bevan's NHS – had clearly not ushered in the perennial one-party state he had feared in 1945. He therefore felt free to undo Labour's mistakes, as he saw them, and build on its achievements, to advance a people more than ready to enjoy the broad(ish), sunlit(ish) uplands it had been promised during the war.

Sarah Churchill had urged her father in 1945 that, since Health was unquestionably Labour's territory now, he should make Housing his. Amid the flurry of messages recalling his old wartime staff to fresh service, Churchill called Harold Macmillan down to Chartwell and asked him to 'Build the houses for the people.'

'I had of course hoped to be Minister of Defence,' Macmillan wrote in his diary, 'But he is determined to keep it in his own hands ... Churchill says it is a gamble – make or mar my political career. But every humble home will bless my name, if I succeed ... but, oh dear, it is not my cup of tea.'

OPPOSITE: Clementine joins Winston for a photo opportunity during the October 1951 general election campaign, which saw the promise – and delivery – of more than a million homes.

In fact, Macmillan was a shrewd appointment and the ambitious target of 300,000 homes a year was surpassed, and most were council houses – a satisfying legacy for the Winston who, 50 years before, had written 'For my own part, I see little glory in an Empire which can rule the waves and is unable to flush its sewers.' The programme of the Tory Party, he told Jock Colville in 1952, must be, 'Houses and meat and not being scuppered' – adding that 'not being broke' was going to be its major difficulty and preoccupation. Houses were done. Meat and bacon finally came off the ration on 4th July 1954. Not being scuppered or broke was a longer-term project, but Churchill would swerve a number of major obstacles before handing back power in 1955.

On 3rd September 1951, Churchill had done 'a thing this morning that I haven't done in many years – I went down on my knees by my bedside & prayed.' The King was desperately ill. On 25th October Winston renewed his role as George VI's Prime Minister but they had barely three months together. On 6th February 1952 the King died in his sleep. He was just 56 years old. It was the

Prime Minister's job to speak to the nation, and Churchill spoke movingly of the last months of the King's life, in which he 'walked with death, as if death were a companion, an acquaintance whom he recognised and did not fear.'

The great wordsmith hand-wrote just two words for the card on the Government wreath for the King's funeral: 'For Valour', the legend on a Victoria Cross, a tribute to their unlikely alliance forged in the dark days of war. What Churchill most cared about now – he would tell the Commons two years into his premiership – was 'the building of a sure and lasting peace'.

The new Queen, at just 25, was in Kenya with her husband when the news came of her father's death. The next day Churchill was there on the tarmac to receive her home, as her father had been to wave her off. 'She is only a child, and I hardly know her,' Churchill said, with tears in his eyes, to Jock Colville when he heard the news. He had, in fact, first met Lilibet when she was just two and a half. She was, he told Clementine at the time, 'a character. She has an air of authority and reflectiveness astonishing in an infant.'

Churchill the historian, of course, heard all the echoes of the young woman who had come to the throne at the same age as her namesake four centuries before: speaking to the nation of the 'Second Queen Elizabeth, also ascending the Throne in her twenty-sixth year,' and reminding Britain, 'Famous have been the reigns of our Queens.' The Crown was, he said, 'the magic link – which unites our loosely bound but strongly interwoven Commonwealth.'

'Commonwealth …' The British Empire that had been Churchill's 'alpha and omega' was no more. Elizabeth would be a Queen, not an Empress. But her genuine enthusiasm for this looser family of states – to which she had pledged her whole life 'whether it be long or short' at the age of 21 – took into a new generation the appreciation of the 'joint inheritance of the English-speaking world and … Magna Carta, the Bill of Rights, the Habeas Corpus, trial by jury, and the English common law,' that Churchill had spoken of at Fulton. India's transition to secular, democratic republic had not been without its tragic consequences. But independent India acknowledged the Queen as 'symbol of the free association of its independent member nations and as such the Head of the Commonwealth', a somewhat nebulous ideal but much in accord with Churchill's own equally nebulous goodwill towards a harmonious and democratic future for all peoples.

OPPOSITE: In 1953 sweet rationing ended and, for the first time in their lives, children could buy as much as they could afford. Meat and all other food came off the ration the following summer.

Churchill told Jock Colville, then in his thirties and back in harness as his Joint Principal Private Secretary, that his younger generation might well witness the end of the Iron Curtain, and he told Nehru he could be 'the light of Asia,' to show all those millions how they can shine out, instead of accepting the darkness of Communism.'

Churchill continued Attlee's policy to develop Britain's own, independent nuclear deterrent – the United States had blocked the sharing of its nuclear secrets with any other nation. Britain's first nuclear test took place in October 1952. Churchill also inherited Labour's ongoing Emergency in Malaya. The British High Commissioner was assassinated by Chinese-backed Communist guerillas just weeks before Churchill came to power. With the military commander sick as well, Churchill appointed Sir Gerald Templer as both. Templer declared on arrival that 'The answer lies not in pouring more troops into the jungle, but in the hearts

ABOVE: Churchill back at his dispatch box as PM. After its 1941 bombing, he had insisted the Commons chamber be rebuilt just as before. He scorned a semi-circular assembly that allowed MPs simply to edge along as their views changed, rather than crossing the floor as he had.

and minds of the Malayan People,' and proved remarkably effective, with many captured guerillas changing sides. The multi-racial Federation of Malay States went on to become independent in 1957.

Churchill's government was also committed to continuing Labour's multi-racial settlement policy in Africa, which meant confronting some of the tough 'rhinoceros questions' he had identified on his 1907 visit to East Africa. His own words had helped to inspire hope for real change and equality in the democracy that all had fought for. Back in 1943, a letter to the *East African Standard* said: 'this is a joint struggle of the black and white people alike. We unreservedly have hurled, and are still hurling ourselves, our efforts, sweat and blood and tears into the war. ... At heart we feel that we deserve fair play when allotment of social, economic, and political goodness is made ... Now is the time for the Government to do real justice and give a chance to Africans.'

In 1952, the decades-long campaign for African rights in Kenya was cut across by the eruption of the murderous campaign of the Land Freedom Army (so-called 'Mau Mau'), which was put down with equal ferocity. However in December 1954, a long meeting with prominent white settler Michael Blundell showed Churchill was unhappy that so many Kenyans were in detention, and he hoped peace talks, even with the Mau Mau, might be a way forward.

Churchill admitted he was old-fashioned on racial matters, but said he had found the Kikuyu people to be 'persons of considerable fibre and ability and steel, who could be brought to our side by just and wise treatment,' while the white settlers were 'a highly individualistic and difficult people'. This he attributed, in part, to the 'tension from the altitude' in the highland areas they dominated.

••• —————— •••

Queen Elizabeth was proving to be the latest in a line of women Winston Churchill allowed gently to keep him in check. The weekly audience between Queen and Prime Minister (at which horse racing – Churchill's post-war passion – was as likely to be discussed as high policy) were punctuated by peals of laughter. Her Prime Minister, the new Queen found, was 'very obstinate' but, like other women in his life, she found ways to handle it.

Churchill advised the Queen against allowing television cameras into Westminster Abbey for her sacred Coronation – the wiser counsel was Prince Philip's, which prevailed. But nevertheless Winston threw himself into preparations for the resplendent Coronation on 2nd June 1953 – 'a signal ... for the brightening

salvation of the human scene'. He attended the
ceremony in full Garter robes, having received
that honour – and become Sir Winston – in the
Queen's Birthday Honours in April. Clemmie,
wrote Colville, really disliked the idea of
giving up being Mrs Churchill. But it was as Sir
Winston and Lady Churchill that they gave, and
attended, a host of Coronation balls and dinners.

Three weeks later, at a dinner for the Italian
Prime Minister, Churchill was taken ill. His
health had for years been a matter for concern –
but this was to prove something altogether graver.

The next morning he presided over a Cabinet
meeting, but had to be guided, tottering, to his
chair before the other ministers arrived, so that no
one would notice how weak he was. That evening
his condition worsened and it became obvious
he had suffered a stroke – his daughter Sarah, summoned home to Chartwell from
New York, said that it was like seeing 'a great oak felled'. Clementine and Colville
were warned he might not survive the weekend; party leaders and Palace discussed

OPPOSITE: Sir Winston and Lady Churchill in robes for the Coronation at Westminster Abbey. The Queen's decision to televise the ceremony, against her Prime Minister's advice, was a triumph.
ABOVE: Elizabeth II also embraced the potential of the rapidly growing Commonwealth, hosting a Commonwealth Conference at which Churchill was now only one of her many Prime Ministers.

SVENSKA AKADEMIEN
HAR VID SAMMANTRÄDE DEN 15 OKTOBER 1953
I ÖVERENSSTÄMMELSE MED FÖRESKRIFTERNA
I DET AV
ALFRED NOBEL
DEN 27 NOVEMBER 1895 UPPRÄTTADE TESTAMENTE
BESLUTAT ATT TILLDELA

sir WINSTON CHURCHILL
1953 ÅRS LITTERÄRA NOBELPRIS
FÖR HANS MÄSTERSKAP I HISTORISK OCH BIO-
GRAFISK FRAMSTÄLLNING SAMT FÖR DEN LYSANDE
TALEKONST MED VILKEN HAN FRAMTRÄTT SOM
FÖRSVARARE AV HÖGA MÄNSKLIGA VÄRDEN.
STOCKHOLM DEN 10 DECEMBER 1953

plans for a caretaker government should he be forced to resign, or worse. His natural successor was Eden – who was also ill and would be out of action for months.

A week later, however, Churchill – the great survivor – began an unexpected recovery. While his son-in-law Christopher Soames and Colville effectively took over his business of government, the public remained in ignorance of his 'temporary incapacity'. Four weeks after the stroke he could leave Chartwell for Chequers and begin to take up work, though still in his daughter Mary's words 'dazed and grey'. Two months later, a letter to Clementine showed him still undecided about the future. But he signed off as her 'loving & as yet unconquered, W.' By December he was well enough to fly to Bermuda for a conference, postponed once already because of his health, with America and France, the other two permanent members of the recently formed North Atlantic Treaty Organisation (NATO). Going to Bermuda meant missing the ceremony for his recent award of the Nobel Prize for Literature, but Clementine went in his place.

Bermuda was the third of Churchill's four post-war visits to America as Prime Minister. He had visited Truman in the last days of his presidency. 'What a pity,' Churchill said to Malcolm Muggeridge in 1950, that Stalin 'has turned out to be

ABOVE: Parliament and Chartwell both feature on Churchill's Nobel Charter Award, 'for his mastery of historical and biographical description as well as for brilliant oratory in defending exalted human values.'

such a swine. Why, he and Truman and Attlee could have ruled the world – what a triumvirate!' Truman's successor was wartime commander Dwight D. Eisenhower, and Churchill had already visited 'Ike' when he was elected but not yet installed. Now in December 1953, and for the rest of his premiership, it was President Eisenhower he had to deal with if he was to nurture the 'special relationship' that was Churchill's only road to world security.

He continued to push for a tripartite rapprochement with the Soviet Union. 'The idea appeals to me of a supreme effort to bridge the gulf between the two worlds, ' he said, 'So that each can live their life if not in friendship, at least without the hatreds and manoeuvres of the Cold War.'

On taking office in 1951, he had sent a friendly greeting to Josef Stalin; on Stalin's death in March 1953 he sent 'regret and sympathy' to the Soviet Union. This change of regime was an opportunity not to be missed and he suggested – unsuccessfully – to Eisenhower a 'Big Three' conference on the lines of Potsdam. He had introduced a new word to the political lexicon that is now so commonplace that few remember that 'summit' is his metaphor: 'It is not easy to see how things can be worsened by a parley at the summit if such a thing were possible.'

His great concern – his last great task, as he saw it – was to preserve the world from nuclear conflict, using the summitry that had won the Second World War and might prevent a Third. The Soviet Union now had its own hydrogen bomb, and Colville's diary recorded that Churchill found Eisenhower 'both weak and stupid' in not seeing the H-bomb 'as something entirely new and terrible,' rather than 'just the latest improvement in military weapons.'

In response to Eisenhower's suggestion in the summer of 1954 that Britain should join America in aiding the French, currently being defeated by Ho Chi Minh's Communist troops in the Vietnam highlands, Churchill wrote 'My Dear Friend … in no foreseeable circumstances' – except possibly local rescue – could Britain's troops be involved. And that 'if we were asked our opinion' the advice to America would be the same. He instead backed a Southeast Asia Treaty Organisation: 'a SEATO, corresponding to NATO in the Atlantic and European sphere. In this it is important to have the support of the Asian countries.'

Churchill was aware that Eden – his friend and ally since his days in the wilderness and through the war years (and now, since 1952, also husband of his brother Jack's girl Clarissa) – was watching him with ever more 'hungry eyes', waiting for him to retire. Eden had been reported as saying that Churchill was 'gaga', and that, 'This simply cannot go on.'

Time and again Churchill had suggested he *would* go, then changed his mind. The Queen for her part declined to use their weekly audience to pressure him. Colville, one of those closest to him, was as undecided as Winston himself: 'still, occasionally, the sparkle of genius could be seen in a decision, a letter, a phrase. But was he the man to negotiate with the Russians and moderate the Americans?'

The volatile state of international affairs had often given Churchill an excuse to cling on to office. In the summer of 1954 he had made his fourth and last US visit as premier – a visit, Colville's diary noted, 'to convince the President that we must co-operate more fruitfully in the atomic and hydrogen sphere and that we, the Americans and British, must go and talk to the Russians in an effort to avert war …' Churchill told Congress: 'Meeting jaw to jaw is better than war.'

In November 1954 Churchill turned 80. On his birthday he spoke in Parliament's ancient Westminster Hall filled with 2,500 people: 'I have never accepted what many people have kindly said: namely that I inspired the nation. It was the nations and the race dwelling all round the globe that had the lion's heart.' He paused. 'I had the luck to be called upon to give the roar.' Perhaps the cheers of the House were a little dampened when curtains were drawn back to reveal the gift of both

Houses – a portrait of Churchill by Graham Sutherland. Churchill hated it (Clementine, later, had it destroyed).

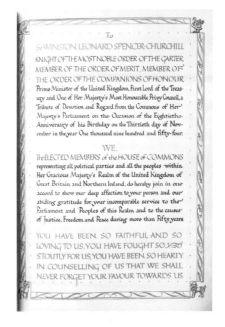

He had floated the idea of marking the occasion by standing down at the general election that would come the following April. Through the winter of 1954–5 he repeatedly told Colville he had lost interest, that he was tired of it all … All the same, he might once again have changed his mind, but he was not given the chance. A few days before Christmas saw a deputation of senior members of the Cabinet confronting Churchill, who said angrily that it was clear they wanted him out. None of them contradicted him. The months of early spring, wrote Mary Soames, were hard going. 'He minds *so* much … It's the first death.'

Anthony Eden would be the next Prime Minister – though Winston wavered again, tempted by a hint that the new Soviet leader Nikolai Bulganin might consider talks. But even Churchill could not delay the inevitable. On 4th April 1955 the Churchills hosted a retirement dinner in Downing Street attended, uniquely, by the Queen and Prince Philip. After the guests had left Colville found Churchill sitting on his bed. The silence was broken when Churchill said, urgently, 'I don't believe Anthony can do it' – leaving Colville to reflect on how often Churchill's pronouncements had proved prophecies.

The following day, when Churchill went to Buckingham Palace to tender his resignation, the Queen offered him, unprecedentedly for many decades, a dukedom. He declined with regret, the more so because she looked so beautiful when she offered it, he said, but decline he did. He would remain the Great Commoner.

OPPOSITE: Graham Sutherland and his wife scrutinise the Churchill portrait during composition. The Edward Ardizzone picture on page 176 was a gift from the Press Gallery.

ABOVE: MPs also signed a leather-bound illuminated address on his birthday – Churchill was genuinely touched by such expressions of affection.

CHAPTER 17

'An iron curtain'

When Churchill left office, at the age of 80, a decade of life still remained to him. Health problems and holidays, and tributes to his lasting prestige, might have been sufficient for most men, but there is a certain inevitability about the fact that he picked up a multi-volume book project, resuming work on his *History of the English-Speaking Peoples*, begun in the 1930s but abandoned when in office. The massive task of writing Winston Churchill's biography – at least the early volumes – would in due course fall to his son Randolph, as Mary would one day write their mother's.

Winston, meanwhile, was looking forward as well as back. In 1959, at Cambridge, he planted a tree on the site of the new Churchill College, which would be his national memorial. One of the first significant works of modern architecture in the country, he wanted it to be modern in another way. John Colville recalled Churchill himself telling the (male) trustees that he hoped the college, with a strong focus on science and technology, would admit women on equal terms with men – this came to pass in 1972 when it was one of the first Oxbridge colleges to do so. Colville asked him if his comment had been Clementine's idea: 'Yes', he said, 'and I support it. When I think what women did in the war I feel sure they deserve to be treated equally.'

In the House of Commons Churchill, sticking to protocol, did not speak in the many debates he attended. But he was perhaps disconcerted to find that Eden – centre stage at last, after so long in the wings – showed no sign of seeking his private guidance either. Asked to issue a public endorsement of Eden's actions over Suez in 1956, he loyally acceded to the request. He was seen in top hat and frock coat a few months later, going to Buckingham Palace to consult on the crisis the invasion of Egypt had precipitated, which eventually caused the collapse of Eden's premiership and ushered in Macmillan's.

OPPOSITE: Churchill, a jaunty feather in his hatband, feeds the golden orfe he introduced to Chartwell. He also introduced its famous black swans, while the mandarin ducks were a gift.

Winston Churchill had often been accused of being too loyal, for too long, to his friends at the expense of his own best interests. He certainly had a lifelong talent for making and keeping friends but, after so long a life, death had inevitably claimed most of them. Early on had come the Great War, where losses included his schoolboy idol at Harrow, Jack Milbanke, who won the Victoria Cross in the Boer War before dying at Gallipoli. His seminal friendship with F.E. Smith, his co-founder of The Other Club, had survived their political differences but not the hard-drinking habits they shared, and Winston had lost F.E. in 1930, on the eve of his wilderness years. Now, in his eighties, Churchill lost another, unexpected, connection that had brought him right into the modern era.

Jack Kennedy, son of Britain's wartime ambassador in 1940, had long been a sincere admirer of Churchill, quoting him nine times during his election campaign. As President John F. Kennedy, he sent a personal greeting on the anniversary of Churchill's signing the Atlantic Charter with Roosevelt, and he made it his personal mission to secure his hero the first honorary American citizenship since Lafayette in 1784.

Sadly, Winston was too ill by April 1963 to cross the Atlantic one last time to receive it from the President himself and sent Randolph in his place, but he and Clementine watched the White House ceremony on television via the Telstar satellite. At the end of that year, he watched again as news reports told of Kennedy's assassination in Dallas, and wept.

The following summer, when yet another old friend, Max Beaverbrook, died, his daughter Sarah (herself recently bereaved when her much-loved third husband died) wrote, 'I grieve for you. No one can give back the golden years of friendship. But remember you have taught me a lot about that. I love you dearly. Your Sarah.'

The family had recently suffered a terrible blow with the death by suicide of Diana, at the age of 54. Clementine was in hospital at the time so Mary had broken the news to her father. 'The lethargy of extreme old age dulls many sensibilities and my father only took in slowly what I had to tell him: but then he withdrew into a great and distant silence.'

It would be a mistake, however, to see the whole of Churchill's last decade as one of unmitigated loss. Winston and Clemmie were fond grandparents of many grandchildren and life at Chartwell often rang with laughter. One of President Kennedy's correspondents told of an afternoon watching a pony that had escaped into the grounds, hotly pursued by its owner, two policemen and the head gardener – while Sir Winston cheered on the pony's bid for freedom.

Animals were, as ever, one of the joys of life at Chartwell for Churchill in his last years. Descendants of his black swans and the mandarin ducks given by Philip Sassoon can still be seen there. So too, probably, can descendants of the butterflies he released from its Butterfly House. He had progressed from the butterfly hunter of childhood to butterfly breeder in middle age, concerned at the decline of native species like the Small Tortoiseshell, Speckled Wood, Peacock and Swallowtail. However his secretary Grace Hamblin recalled him flinging the door open one day, setting them free with the words, 'I can't bear this captivity any longer!'

She also recalled his kindness on the death of his brown poodle Rufus, of whom she had become extremely fond. A second Rufus would come to Chartwell eventually, but Churchill's first thought was to arrange for her to have a puppy of her own.

Churchill's early ambitions to be a gentleman farmer had foundered on his reluctance to kill or eat any animal to whom he had recently bid 'Good morning!',

OPPOSITE: A favourite family photograph shows Winston and Clementine with five of their grandchildren – the kittens of their kittens, enjoying the pleasures of Chartwell in their turn.
ABOVE: As well as Rufus II, Winston loved his marmalade cats. He stipulated Chartwell must always have a marmalade cat in residence, called Jock after Jock Colville, and with white bib and four white socks. Jock VI arrived in 2014.

and when a Chartwell fowl was served at the table, it was often Clementine who had to carve it. Later, he valued the different breeds of cattle on the farms that he had now been able to add to the estate and his daughters persuaded him to rescue two goats from a Gypsy encampment. But he was particularly attached to his pigs. Dogs look up to humans, he said, and cats look down, but pigs 'treat us as equals'.

As well as his life in Chartwell and London, Winston spent more and more time away from Britain, in the sunshine, thanks in large part to three of his friends. It was at Lord Beaverbrook's villa La Capponcina, near Monte Carlo, that he and Clementine celebrated their Golden Wedding anniversary in 1958. Their children gave them a spectacular album of rose paintings by leading artists, together with the avenue of golden rose bushes that is still a feature of Chartwell. Another frequent destination was La Pausa, 10 miles away, a villa originally built by the Duke of Westminster for Coco Chanel and now owned by Winston's millionaire agent Emery Reves, who took care to invite dinner guests Winston would find interesting. But Clementine was most likely to agree to join her husband aboard *Christina*, yacht of Aristotle Onassis, on which they cruised in company with assorted Churchill relations and a cast of celebrities from Maria Callas to Margot Fonteyn.

Clementine persuaded Winston, at last, to retire from Parliament when his old seat was abolished in boundary changes in 1964. His last recorded words in the Chamber, two years earlier – in response to the good wishes of the House on his birthday – had been, perfectly appropriately, 'I am very grateful to you all.'

The month after his retirement he celebrated his 90th birthday – quietly, but with a crowd gathering outside his London home to sing 'Happy Birthday'.

He had already visited Chartwell for the last time. On 24th January 1965 – 70 years to the day after the death of his father – Winston Churchill died. Tributes poured in from around the globe. The President of India wrote to Elizabeth II that he had been 'the greatest Englishman we have known' and the Queen wrote to Clementine that the world had been made 'poorer by the loss of his many-sided genius'. The *New York Times* obituary told America that 'The great figure who embodied man's will to resist tyranny passed into history this morning.' For the world too, it was 'the end of an age'. Labour Prime Minister Harold Wilson paid tribute, speaking of 'a life in which he created history and which will be remembered as long as history is read.'

The Queen had long directed that Winston Churchill would be accorded a state funeral; the first such given to a commoner for almost 70 years. The plan, codenamed 'Operation Hope Not' went perfectly. For three days Churchill's body lay in state in Westminster Hall with four soldiers, heads bowed, around his coffin. More than 300,000 people filed past to pay their respects, the queues stretching back two miles in the freezing cold.

A team of naval ratings pulled a gun carriage bearing his body through crowded streets to St Paul's Cathedral. The Queen herself set aside precedence by arriving before the coffin, and instructed family members not to bow or curtsy as they passed her. After the service, the body was taken by boat along the Thames towards Waterloo Station and, famously, the great cranes along the river were dipped as it passed by, while fighter jets dipped their wings overhead. From Waterloo, a special train carried the coffin towards Blenheim, and, as Winston had requested, to an unassuming resting place in the cemetery at Bladon, the burial ground of the Churchill family.

Many years before, Churchill had visited his father's grave there and wrote to his mother of the beauty and restfulness of the spot. 'The hot sun of the last few days has dried up the grass a little – but the rose bushes are in full bloom and make the churchyard very bright. I was so struck by the sense of quietness & peace as well as by the old world air of the place.'

Winston Churchill's grave was marked only by a simple stone giving the dates of his life – and, once her ashes were interred beside him, those of his wife Clementine too. Visitors ever since have commented on the fact that there is no more – but the truth, of course, is that there is far too much for any monument to say.

OPPOSITE: Winston introduced buddleia or 'butterfly bush' to Chartwell, thought to be one of the oldest wildlife gardens in the country.
ABOVE: A modest stone greets the visitor to the 'quietness and peace' of Bladon churchyard where Winston Churchill is buried – about a mile away from the palace where he was born.
OVERLEAF: The dipping of the wharfside cranes as Churchill's coffin passed, even more than the fly-past overhead, remains an abiding memory for anyone who witnessed it.

Places to Visit

Chartwell, near Westerham, Kent (National Trust)

Winston's beloved home of so many years offers both many insights into Churchill the man and a new appreciation of his achievements. Inside the house, many rooms are left as he and Clementine would have known them. Others are used as museum space, hosting changing exhibitions and a permanent display including items from the trophy cups won by his racehorses to one of his famous 'siren suits'.

Outside in the extensive gardens, visitors can see descendants of the black swans he ordered for the lake and the golden orfe he painted in their fishponds; the brick walls he built with his own hands and the butterflies he bred. As well as the 'Marycot', the charming miniature house made for his daughter, it is possible to visit his painting studio crammed with his own works.

www.nationaltrust.org.uk/chartwell

Blenheim Palace, Woodstock, Oxfordshire

The ancestral home of the Spencer-Churchill family is remarkable for the sheer scale of Vanbrugh and Hawksmoor's early eighteenth-century design. The grandeur of the state rooms with their portraits and porcelain, their priceless bibelots, contrasts with the unassuming room where Winston was born.

Outside, in the vast grounds landscaped by Capability Brown, is the little Grecian temple where Churchill proposed to Clementine. St Martin's Church at Bladon, on the edge of the Blenheim estate, holds the simple grave they share.

www.blenheimpalace.com

The Houses of Parliament, Westminster, London

If Chartwell was his home and Blenheim represented his heritage, then the Houses of Parliament – scene of his triumphs and defeats, seat of the democracy he served – held another huge piece of Churchill's heart.

When the House is sitting, anyone can queue and go through the strict security to walk through Westminster Hall, the oldest part of the Palace of Westminster.

Entry to the gallery above the famous green benches of the Commons Chamber to hear a debate is naturally limited, but it is also possible to listen to Lords debates and Committees.

When Parliament is not sitting, tickets for a tour, guided or audio, also allows you see these and other parts of the building. British visitors can also visit Westminster by arrangement with their MP. Note: the planned restoration may change these arrangements.

www.parliament.uk/visiting

Churchill War Rooms, Westminster, London

The Cabinet War Rooms (as they were originally known) were set up just before World War II as an underground command centre easily accessible from Downing Street. Today, there is nothing more evocative than to walk through the cramped complex, arranged as it would have been, where every detail tells a story, from the Map Room where the war was plotted to the tiny cabinet where a secure radio-telephone line put the British Prime Minister in touch with the American President. From the spartan bedroom where Churchill would snatch an afternoon nap, to the scratch marks on the arms of his chair and the candles waiting ready for when electricity went out. Queues to visit can be long, so pre-booking is recommended.

www.iwm.org.uk/visits/churchill-war-rooms

Westminster College, Fulton, Missouri, USA

It seems fitting that the half-American Churchill should also be honoured across the Atlantic, and the American National Churchill Museum and study centre in Fulton, where he made his famous 'iron curtain' speech, houses a huge collection of pictures, correspondence and Churchilliana. The site also boasts the seventeenth-century church of St Mary Aldermanbury, designed by Sir Christopher Wren, which once stood in the City of London. Gutted in the Blitz, it was shipped to Fulton stone by stone, to be lovingly rebuilt in Churchill's memory.

www.nationalchurchillmuseum.org

Further Reading

There are, according to distinguished Churchill biographer Andrew Roberts, more than one thousand biographies of Winston Churchill currently available. There is, therefore, no shortage of choice for those who wish to discover more about the man. The only question is where to start. Given that one entire book addresses just five days of his life, while another focuses on just 12 minutes, this could become a never-ending journey …

Winston's own *My Early Life* (Eland Publishing and other editions) introduces the reader not only to his views on the events of his first three decades but to his most witty and engaging writing. His other books and journalism, encompassing many millions of words, then lie ahead if you wish to take that path.

Churchill's youngest daughter Mary edited her parents' letters to one another over a lifetime in *Speaking for Themselves: The Personal Letters of Winston and Clementine*. Lady Soames also filled in the family picture from the other side of the marriage in a number of volumes including *Clementine Churchill* (Doubleday and other editions).

Randolph S. Churchill wrote the first two volumes of the monumental authorised biography of his father: *Winston S. Churchill* (Heinemann and other editions) gives the most comprehensive account of the public life. The project was taken over after Randolph's death by an assistant recruited in 1962, historian Martin Gilbert. After completion of the eighth and final volume, Gilbert published supporting documents, with more volumes appearing after his own death in 2015. Sir Martin Gilbert's single volume *Churchill: A Life* encapsulates a lifetime of Churchill scholarship.

Beyond these, there are too many excellent and illuminating one, two or three-volume biographies to make it possible to list them here. But surely Winston Churchill himself, keen reader of science fiction, would be thrilled to know the internet offers the chance to witness all his contributions to debates in the Commons (except the wartime Secret Sessions). These, recorded by the copy-takers of *Hansard*, are now made available online at api.parliament.uk/historic-hansard/people/mr-winston-churchill.

The authors would like to thank the following people: Michael Bishop, Katie Bond, Katherine Carter, Nicole Day, Amy Feldman, Niall Harman, Dr Jerzy Kierkuc-Bielinski, Nicola Newman, Beatrice Rapley, Peter Taylor, Gordon Wise.

Credits

Index